Konstantin Stanislavsky by Bella Merli
Hijikata Tatsumi and Ohno Kazuo
    Tamah Nakamura
Mary Wigman by Mary Ann Santos N
Robert Wilson by Maria Shevtsova

Future volumes will include:

Marina Abramović
Antonin Artaud
Peter Brook
Tadeusz Kantor
Richard Schechner

I've always believed – even before I was working with the Repère Cycles or this method of working we have now – that writing starts the night that you start performing. Before that, at what people usually call rehearsals, we structure and improvise. The writing should be the last thing we do. In theater it should be the traces of what you've done on stage ... The whole notion of 'playing' in theatre has been evacuated in this century. I think that the people who are part of our company are not interested in acting that much they are interested in playing.

Lepage in McAlpine, 1996, 135

ROBERT LEPAGE

Aleksandar Saša Dundjerović

LONDON AND NEW YORK

First published 2009
by Routledge
2 Park Square, Milton Park, Abingdon, Oxon OX14 4RN

Simultaneously published in the USA and Canada
by Routledge
270 Madison Avenue, New York, NY 10016

Routledge is an imprint of the Taylor & Francis Group, an informa business

Typeset in Perpetua
by Taylor & Francis Books
Printed and bound in Great Britain
by TJ International Ltd, Padstow, Cornwall

British Library Cataloguing in Publication Data
A catalogue record for this book is available from the British Library

Library of Congress Cataloging in Publication Data
 Dundjerović, Aleksandar Saša, 1965–
 Robert Lepage / Aleksandar Saša Dundjerović.
  p. cm. — (Routledge performance practitioners)
 Includes bibliographical references and index.
 1. Lepage, Robert—Criticism and interpretation. I. Title.
 PN2308.L46D85 2008
 792'.0233092—dc22

                                        2008025941

ISBN10: 0-415-37519-3 (hbk)
ISBN10: 0-415-37520-7 (pbk)
ISBN10: 0-203-09897-8 (ebk)

ISBN13: 978-0-415-37519-1 (hbk)
ISBN13: 978-0-415-37520-7 (pbk)
ISBN13: 978-0-203-09897-4 (ebk)

CONTENTS

FIGURES

ACKNOWLEDGEMENTS

The contents of this book are based upon my PhD thesis on Lepage's theatre, my previous book *The Theatricality of Robert Lepage* and teaching students over the last fifteen years in directing and devising. I am thankful to a great number of people for helping me on this journey.

I would like to express my gratitude to my editor Franc Chamberlain for his support and valuable comments that enormously helped me in compiling this book. I am thankful to Professor David Bradby under whose supervision I started my research on Robert Lepage's directing practice. Thanks too to staff at Routledge for help in making this project come together. I am grateful to a number of people associated with *Ex Machina* who have helped me over the years of my research, but particularly to Robert Lepage, Linda Beaulieu, Michel Bernatchez, Michael Morris and Micheline Beaulieu – archivist from *Ex Machina* – for her time and understanding. My heartfelt thanks goes to my circle of readers and commentators – Rémy Charest, Tracy Lea, Meretta Elliot, Sarah Meadows, Christine Carson and Teodora Dundjerović.

During the past ten years I have worked with many students, exploring Lepage's devising and workshop process, at Royal Holloway, University of London; Brunel University; The University of Manchester; and The University of Sao Paulo, Brazil. I am thankful to all of them for their participation and insight. I am particularly grateful to Rodrigo Garcez for his help with the images in Chapter 4.

Finally, I would like to dedicate this book to my wife, Ilva Navarro Bateman, and express my gratitude to my father Professor Dr Aleksandar Dundjerović.

CULTURAL AND ARTISTIC BIOGRAPHY: ROBERT LEPAGE IN-BETWEEN WORLDS

INTRODUCTION

Robert Lepage is one of the world's foremost theatre directors, and is widely regarded as a key contemporary performance visionary. He is a director, playwright/deviser, actor and multi-media artist whose performance practice combines various artistic forms, traditions and cultures. The theatre is only one of the media used by Lepage. He also works as a film *auteur* and directs opera, rock concerts, installations and large spectacle performances – notably his directing of *KA* in 2004, a $200 million production for the **Cirque du Soleil** in Las Vegas. Lepage connects popular culture with high-art aestheticism, through a visually engaging theatricality made for people dissatisfied with traditional text-based theatre. He challenges the audience's understanding of the theatre performance as a finished and complete artistic act through his work-in-progress approach, which is developmental, open and one of continuous transformation. Consequently, Lepage views performance as rehearsal and rehearsal as performance – blurring the difference between the two, he often uses the term 'open' or 'public rehearsal' for performance.

Lepage's theatre connects a number of important late twentieth- and early twenty-first-century performance practitioners, such as **Jacques Lecoq, Peter Brook, Pina Bausch** and **Laurie Anderson**. Lepage's theatre inspires new practitioners, directors, actors and scholars alike, and the process of his work is studied at universities worldwide. In spite of this there are very few studies of his work, and even fewer which examine his creative process. The reason for this is that Lepage is very prolific as a **director-author**. As he makes three or four major projects a year, any study of his work can only temporarily be bound by the date that the material is published. Moreover, Lepage is a practitioner who creates live theatre performance and not a written text. Textual or video recordings of his performances are limited, but there has been a more organized approach since the conceptualization of La Caserne in 1997, his home-based performance lab in Quebec City. Lepage is not interested in theatre as a pedagogue, nor is he setting up his own 'system' of work to be studied by others. In fact, he contradicts the view that there is any method to his work practice, although there is a very recognizable director's 'signature' in all of his productions. He does not write about his understanding of theatre and until now the only account of his work is given in *Robert Lepage – Connecting Flights* (1997), a book of interviews with Rémy Charest.

Lepage's real influence lies in his creative process rather than the product, regardless of its accomplishment. He is important for an understanding of the liveness and immediacy of contemporary performance, because of the way he uses all of the theatre production elements (making a **mise-en-scène** into a main medium for narration), and the belief that theatre art could encompass all other art forms. Lepage's work proposes that meaning in the theatre is found in the relationship between every element (the sum of all the different parts) of theatre production, not just the text or the actor. His focus is on understanding performance as a rehearsal – a performance is not a fixed form, but alive. It is 'presenting work that [is] "unfinished", expecting and ready to integrate or reflect audience response' (Heddon and Milling, 2006, 21). Similarly to **Anna Halprin**, whose teaching of *The RSVP Cycles* Lepage adopted, he emphasizes the process and not the achievement of a final product. In the tradition of **Jean Cocteau**, Lepage is a multi-disciplinary artist who also brings different art forms (live performance, and film in particular) together in a montage. In **total theatre** the equal emphasis is on all elements rather than verbal language. Lepage's theatre is founded on the **dramaturgy** of visual images and actors' performativity, through which he wants to achieve global communication that will not be inhibited by the audience's inability to understand the productions' verbal language.

STORYTELLING AND LANGUAGES

Robert Lepage was born in Quebec City, Quebec, Canada on 12 December 1957, into a typical working-class French Canadian family. One of four children, his mother was a housewife and his father a cab driver. What made Lepage's family unusual was that they were bi-lingual. Lepage's mother had lived in London during the Second World War and his father had been in the Royal Navy, and during that time they had become fluent in English. Initially unable to have children, they adopted two English-speaking children. Some years after the adoption, Robert and his sister were born. In their home English and French language co-existed simultaneously and were constantly mixed. Lepage liked to see his family with its bi-lingual mix as 'a metaphor for Canada, a cultural metaphor' (Lepage, 2002). His bi-lingual upbringing was exceptional in the francophone cultural environment that was Quebec City.

The concern for language and communication in Lepage's theatre emerged in response both to the cultural duality (English and French) in Canada and to two opposing forces   those of the isolationism of **Quebec's nationalist politics**, and the internationalist Quebeckers who needed to connect to the world and get out of its linguistic enclosure. Lepage is aware that if Québécois theatre is to be understood and 'to have access to the market, to be invited all over the world', it has to overcome the limitations of language. As he explains: 'You have to do this extra effort to get the story clear, to illustrate it, to give another layer to it' (McAlpine, 1996, 150). This need to translate and the urgency to be understood forced theatre authors in Quebec to invent a theatricality based on visual images, sound, music and a physical expression that was able to communicate beyond the constraints of verbal language.

Growing up in Quebec City in the 1960s and 1970s, Lepage felt the powerful impacts of clerical nationalism, conservative ideology and the dominance of white French Catholics over all aspects of life, in particular family and cultural politics. The Anglophone minority in Quebec was mainly centred in Montreal, and had economic power. The francophone majority lived mostly on farms, while the working class lived in the cities. Since Lepage's family was bi-lingual, he could not fully identify with a dominant francophone centre. This cultural and linguistic position meant that Lepage did not belong to either of the two groups. Combined with his sexual ambiguity and his alopecia (the loss of body hair that he suffered at the age of six) this made his childhood difficult, and as a result he was somewhat reclusive, shy and prone to depression (Lepage, 2002). He became an outsider in his own cultural context, assuming the position of **otherness**. It was in the theatre that Lepage found a place of escape where he could assume alternative identities, exorcize his fears and engage with his own personal problems. The questioning of language, of human communication, and the stability of identity and going out of one's own location into other cultures to find answers to one's own dilemmas are dominating themes in Lepage's theatre. In fact, all of his theatre and films are shaped through the conflict between a local (inner) and international (outer) perspective, by exposing Quebec's local character to the world and outside influences.

When he was a child, Lepage's mother often told him war stories about Europe and life in old Quebec City. The stories were personal recollections of the past, distorted through the lens of memory and transformed through time. It was this imprecision and embellishment, rather than their accuracy, that attracted Lepage to the oral tradition of storytelling. He has said that in order to create, one has to be a mytho-maniac: 'You have to be able to amplify the stories you hear, give a large dimension to stories you invent. This is how you transform them into legends and myths' (Charest, 1997, 19). At the same time, Lepage's childhood fascination with the stories his father made up on the trips he organized for tourists around Quebec City had a significant influence on Lepage's own storytelling in the theatre. He would accompany his father and listen to stories that were an intoxicating mix of local myth, fiction and fact, and that were often adapted according to the occasion and who the spectators/tourists were. Lepage uses his childhood sense of wonder and the discovery of the unknown in telling his stories through the theatre. Each of his projects inevitably deals with a main character going into a new country or environment, and discovering something about themselves in the new location that significantly changes their life.

Lepage's favourite subject in school was geography. As he points out, all his work in the theatre relates to geography, travelling and cultural differences between countries. It is 'not just going to Europe in a plane, it's also the geography of the human environment and what that means and how does it have an influence?' (Dundjerović, 2003, 153). His version of **intercultural** theatre has the naïvety of a first discovery, of travel to a new destination and stories told about a journey that is always transposed through a personal memory and perspective. It was hardly a coincidence that Lepage's main fascination with the theatre was as a live, improvised and unstructured performance, where the actor-creator (often Lepage himself) gives a personal account of events and establishes their own relationship with the stories, thus creating what is known in performance as 'auto-mythologies'.

All of Lepage's stories sit at the local and the global cultural intersection, where the personal is confronted with outside perceptions. His theatre is created in Quebec City for the purpose of global touring, to go to audiences across the world from London and Paris to Sydney and Tokyo. However, his theatre performances remain profoundly influenced by Québécois social and cultural references. Lepage's *mise-en-scène* creates a debate between and interaction with national identity and internationalism, individual and collective creation, local and global references, and live and recorded media. Within the **postmodern** context, his theatre exists between worlds (cultures, art forms, identities, territories, narratives, destinations) and through the interface of live and subjective with recorded and collective experiential process.

Lepage's performance practice reinforces **Roland Barthes**' idea of mythologies in contemporary life, where everything has its form of narrative and that, in contemporary culture, we are surrounded with a plurality of narratives rather then one main narrative (Barthes, 1993). In this way, a culture is the sum of the narratives arranged in social patterns that we have experience of, that we accept, and with which we can identify. This also means that narratives are subjective and flexible so that they can be re-ordered according to memory and personal interpretation. Lepage invariably affirms that the veracity or preservation of a story is not important. What *is* important is how the story interacts with the outside world and how those who interpret it give it its actualization. Subjectivity in Lepage's creative process has a central place; his storytelling is a way of telling audiences about himself. In order to find out who he is, Lepage has to define himself in the context of the outside world. He takes up the position of a storyteller, he uses all the apparatus of various theatrical elements to relate to and communicate with an international audience. In the writing of the story as well as its presentation Lepage uses public rehearsals in front of an audience, whose presence helps in the discovery of the actual structure of the performance narratives.

The motivation to explore language as sound is an outcome of the cultural politics of Quebec's linguistic isolation, as well as Lepage's reclusive personality. Lepage acknowledges that linguistic problems are the main issue with which Quebec artists have to deal, and they need to find a way to get their ideas across if the audience does not understand their language. In a 1991 census only 25% of Canada's population spoke French, and the majority of these people were located in Quebec. As a result, 'the seventies and eighties saw a widespread move away from text-centred theatre' (Jacobson, 1991, 18). Quebec's language isolation and politics of nationalism was a concern shared by a number of other theatre companies working there in the 1980s and 1990s. They had to use touring models as well as non-verbal theatre to reach audiences outside of Quebec and even more so outside of Canada. The goal of Québécois collective theatre and performance groups was to create a means of communication that was unobstructed by the limitations of verbal language, and so enable them to communicate cross-culturally. Other internationally renowned Quebec companies, such as **Carbone 14**, **LaLaLa Human Steps** and Cirque du Soleil, all developed ways of communicating in their own performance style that overcame the obstacles of cultural politics, language and geographical location to attract international audiences. In the work of Carbon 14, 'the "concrete" language of the stage (corporal movement, music, light and other scenographic elements) is understood as more important than spoken language for the purposes of creating and communicating meaning' (Wallace, 1990, 190).

Replacing text and verbal language with a concrete language of the stage is central to Lepage's theatricality. It is an expression founded on the performers' engagement with space, objects and the body, creating a mode of communication that is free from verbal language. It is important to note that, while the Québécois cultural context (particularly the quest for national identity) inevitably influenced Lepage, his theatrical language was a communication tool that he used on a more personal level to escape loneliness and isolation. He adopted the existing discourse of theatrical language in the broadest sense, appropriating the new 'corporeal language' without political or ideological references. He built theatricality on discourses created from verbal and non-verbal utterance, comprising visual elements such as gestures, mime, movement, space, properties (objects) and light.

To explain this shift in emphasis, Lepage points to the political function of language in Montreal and Quebec City:

> Words were so coloured with politics, at least in the 1970s, that people turned to non-verbal theatre to try and get other messages across. Politics were so present in Canadian life in the 1970s that a lot of the creative work in Canada was based only on the politics of the mind, not the politics of the body, of emotions, or of relationships. I think an artist sometimes has to put words aside, to explore these types of politics.
>
> (Huxley and Witts, 1996, 239)

The linguistic situation prompted Lepage to provide an answer by working within the scope of bi-lingual or multi-lingual productions, emphasizing language as sound and working with the performers' physical and vocal expression, separated from narrative or textual structures. Words as sounds are resources (theatrical objects with which the performer can play). 'To me and the actors I work with, the performance is what's most important. Words are sometimes just a way of saying music' (Jacobson, 1991, 19). Mixing languages and projecting their translation, making a simultaneous collage of different languages (English, French, Italian, German, Serbo-Croatian, Chinese, Japanese, etc.) and using language as a sound or as music rather than as a locus of meaning can be a key element in the performance *mise-en-scène*.

Although Lepage's performances are often theoretically situated within intercultural theatre, they are as much about the collision of cultures and linguistic misunderstandings as cultural exchanges. This relates to Lepage's experience of the Canadian dual identity. However, his theatre is pertinent to a global reading and has themes that are accessible to interpretation by other cultures outside the Canadian experience. This is because his theatre appeals to the urban cosmopolitan audience which is exposed to cultural collisions and a plurality of perspectives. The interpretation of his plays is open – it allows the audience to create their own meaning, and to indirectly influence the further development of a performance which Lepage refers to as a work in progress. This ability to change and evolve a performance while touring comes from the tradition of improvised theatre. The plurality of perceptions in Lepage's performance narrative emerges not only from the tensions between the local and the global, but also from personal and collective improvisations. Lepage's theatricality focuses on the interaction and interconnection between the performer and the spectators, where the performer does not follow a fixed narrative but is open to discovery in front of the audience. Lepage's collaborative

method invites continuous debate between individual and group creation, and allows for substantial creative input from the actor as the
author of the performance.

Many different perspectives are also achieved through the plurality
of media used for storytelling. **Peter Gabriel** was an important
influence on Lepage in the 1970s, with rock group Genesis using
theatrical influences and mixing media. Genesis created in 1974 the
rock opera *The Lamb Lies Down on Broadway*, mixing rock with live
performance, masks, projections of films and slides. It was not traditional theatre that had an impact on young Lepage, but theatricality.
As he explains, the influence came 'from seeing rock shows, dance
shows and performance art, then from seeing theatre ...' (1992, 242).
Lepage has always been attracted to working with collaborators from
different media – each bringing their own artistic vocabulary and
skills – and combining this with live performance to provide the
necessary mixture of live and recorded theatricality.

APPRENTICE (1978–84)

In 1975, at the age of 17, Lepage was admitted to the Conservatoire
d'art dramatique de Québec, which was the main training school for
professional actors in Quebec City. Students had to be at least 18
years old and have a high-school diploma. Lepage had abandoned his
high-school education and he lied about his diploma. His inexperience
and youth were seen as positive aspects in the audition, and he was
accepted. The Conservatoire had a fairly rigid programme, which followed the tradition of professional theatre schools training actors for
the demands of the industry. Students were taught with very specific
acting techniques and, consequently, used the tools (and clichés) of
psychological realism that were so dominant in the TV, film and
theatre industries of the 1970s. At the Conservatoire Lepage could
not subscribe to one specific style of acting. His performances did not
follow one technique, but were eclectic and diversified. Furthermore,
as a performer, Lepage was working more on the action and energy
produced in performance than on emotion and psychological realism.

> At the Conservatoire, I was taught a definition of emotion, which I learned
> but never managed to produce on stage. And for three years, I was told that I
> acted without emotion. Right from my very first professional shows, however,

I managed to move the audience. I didn't really understand what made this happen and it took me a long time before I begun to sort it out, before I could really distinguish the difference between the emotion that an actor feels on the stage and the energy he needs to generate that emotion in the audience.

(Charest, 1997, 155)

Lepage's training as an actor was held back by his inability to reproduce 'ordinary' realistic scenes acted with emotional engagement and psychological involvement, as required by the realistic, character-based actor training methods. However, creating emotional response in the audience is not the same as actors feeling psychological emotions. What had a big influence on Lepage at the Conservatoire was working on physical improvisations and character observations, through the limited exposure he had to Jacques Lecoq's techniques in movement classes that were taught by one of Lecoq's former students, Marc Doré. In fact, Doré encouraged Lepage to explore techniques using the body, space and everyday objects. The Lecoq exercises that had the most impact on Lepage were movement improvisations and the observation of everyday situations.

After graduating from the Conservatoire in 1978, Lepage and his classmate Richard Fréchette were the only graduates who were unemployed. They did not have an agent, and realized that they would have to start their own company if they wanted to work. In the summer of that year they went to Paris and joined **Alain Knapp**'s workshop at his *Institut de la personnalité créatrice* for three weeks. The workshops taught actors how to become the creators of their performance by working simultaneously as directors and writers. The sessions were based on Knapp's artistic philosophy of teaching the actor to write their own performance text, rather than to be an interpreter of someone else's work. The actors would write, perform and direct their own material as well as working on all aspects of production-making. In Knapp's workshop, Lepage learned how to devise theatre. For Lepage, the most important aspect of Knapp's workshop was that it gave him an awareness of his own ability to work in many different ways as actor, writer and director, and that it was good to be eclectic. By working in this way he was able to turn what were formerly considered to be his faults in the Conservatoire (reserve, control and a plurality of styles) into a personal style for creating a performance.

When Lepage returned from Paris, he founded Théâtre Hummm ... with Richard Fréchette, working as actor and director, adapting plays and writing his own performance texts. The company existed for a year, and mainly toured schools and local arts venues in towns around Quebec City. Two years later, in 1980, Lepage was asked by Jacques Lessard, one of his teachers from the Conservatoire, to take part in a collectively created performance – *L'école, c'est secondaire* (*School, it's secondary*) – for Quebec City's newly established experimental theatre company, Théâtre Repère. Returning from a year-long study with Anna Halprin in San Francisco, Lessard had gathered together several graduates of the Conservatoire in 1979 and founded Théâtre Repère, using Halprin's *The RSVP Cycles* as a creative method for theatre performance. In short, Lessard argued that the collective creative theatre in Quebec had reached a situation of stalemate, that it lacked any creative system able to produce its own structure, could not be used to make ideologically driven text and, in fact, less successfully replicated Quebecker text-based theatre.

The initials 'RSVP' – meaning please respond – are used not as an indication of any structure, but to suggest communication, an invitation to the audience to respond. This creative process was conceived by Lawrence and Anna Halprin. Lawrence was a landscape architect and environmental planner. His wife Anna was a dancer, choreographer and director of the Dancers' Workshop in San Francisco. Together they put together in the late 1960s the theory-practice of *The RSVP Cycles*, utilizing their own combined experiences with environmental design/space and dance theatre/body. This work process became extremely influential in helping to increase human creative potentials. *The RSVP Cycles* can be adapted to any human creative process and have a varied application, not only in dance and performance but in psychology and therapy. The word 'cycles' refers to a cyclical form where human action is a cycle and the creative process can start from any point within the cycle. *The RSVP Cycles* are founded on (r)esources, (s)cores, (v)aluaction and (p)erformance – which in dance and performance are space, objects and the body, placing improvisation at the core of the creative process.

However, Lessard perceived that theatre performance requires a greater emphasis on the actors' form of expression and on the sequential organization of the working process. He re-worked *The RSVP Cycles*, making them a central pre-occupation of his Théâtre Repère. In

French *repère* means reference or landmark point. At the core of the work process is a performer who establishes a personal reference point with the material that is devised. Repère demonstrates the effect of reducing the importance of words and increasing the importance of other theatrical forms of expression, such as movement, light, sound, objects, etc. As Lessard indicates, 'The Cycles Repère are an extremely precious working instrument which gives the creator a tool, without limiting the liberty of imagination and sensibility' (Roy, 1993, 31–32).

After their initial collaboration, in 1982 Lepage was invited by Lessard to direct and perform in *En Attendant (Awaiting)*, about young artists in a sate of limbo waiting to get a break with their careers. In the same year he and Richard Fréchette both joined the Théâtre Repère as full members. The emphasis in *En Attendant* was on one simple situation and image rather than words and narrative. Lessard, Lepage and Fréchette manipulated physical objects through games, using improvisations and playing a range of characters. The set was simple with Oriental references (a backdrop painted with Japanese characters was the key image). Props and costumes were transformed by being used in different ways. For example, a simple chair had many uses depending on the needs of the actor/character at any given time. In fact, *En Attendant* was a collective creation containing the origins of basic theatrical inclinations that would eventually become the foundations of Lepage's theatrical vocabulary.

Another important influence on the development of Lepage's practice was his experience with **La Ligue Nationale d'Improvisation** (LNI), which he joined in 1984. The idea behind LNI was not only to be a Québécois version of **Keith Johnstone**'s Theatresports, but to revitalize the local theatre by bringing in actors with different experiences to engage in improvisations in the manner of a sporting competition, through a game, and therefore making the theatre a more active and unpredictable place. It was also serving as a place where actors could practise and perform in front of live audiences. Actors were invited to tell their stories and improvise their sessions in a way similar to that of stand-up comedians, surrounded by an audience in an area set up like a hockey ring.

Lepage as actor was excellent in short improvisations, and had already been performing short improvisations for Théâtre Repère in small local theatres as part of a one-night bill of solo acts. Here, in 1984, Lepage received his first critical recognition as a performer by winning the O'Keefe trophy for the actor awarded the most stars for solo improvisations, and the Pierre-Curzi award for recruit of the year at the LNI. Through these improvisation sessions Lepage learned to use all the external elements from outside reality (most importantly audience presence) as personal resources (stimuli) to play with. He explored ways of improvising from 'peripheral consciousnesses'. This is the ability to take all of the surrounding elements of the actor's environment and incorporate them into the improvisation as stimuli to respond to. For example, any accident or spontaneous unplanned moment that the performer becomes conscious of (even outside events, such as noises from the street, things that happened before rehearsal, or cultural/political happenings at the time) can be used as material from which to improvise.

EXPLORING FORMS: THÉÂTRE REPÈRE (1984–91)

Lepage's involvement with Théâtre Repère subsequently shaped the form and direction of the development of his theatrical style. In Canada in the early 1980s, when Lepage started to work in collective creations, it was important to find a new form of expression which would be different from text-based verbal theatre. The development of new technology and communications led to the breakdown of the barriers between different media and the arts. This was followed by an increased interest in and borrowing from other traditions (particularly from the East), that opened the possibilities for new hybrid art forms to be created. The plurality of artistic forms in Lepage's performances reflects a collective creative tradition of using all available elements to create a production. We can also see his work in the context of a postmodern unification of visual disciplines (film, paintings, pop videos, internet and advertising) into one visual culture (Mirzoeff, 1999, 139). Regardless of the media he employs, Lepage embodies the postmodern position of author as editor, gathering various stimuli into a montage of performance experiences.

Lepage's main role in Théâtre Repère was not as a performer but as director. He directed collectively created material and edited improvised solo or group material into a performance. In 1984 he acted in and directed Théâtre Repère's devised project *Circulations*, after which he became responsible for devising new touring projects. He began working on experimental projects with a group of performers as a separate wing within Théâtre Repère, re-creating and representing the world that interested him – a world that existed in-between dreams, memories, reality and fantasy, and was theatrically expressed through visual images. This way of making theatre and communicating about the world found its audience in the 1980s.

After the success of *Circulations,* the work in Théâtre Repère was divided into two areas. Jacques Lessard was concerned with the pedagogy and training of actors who could work through the Repère Cycles, with its very strict creative system, while Lepage was an artistic director responsible for explorations of storytelling through theatrical forms. For Lepage, this period with Théâtre Repère was marked by the search for his own directing style and technique. He explained that, coming to Théâtre Repère, he 'united Jacques Lessard's creative theories about the Repère Cycles with the intuitive method that we [Lepage and Fréchette] were using in our shows' (Charest, 1997, 139).

Devising performance material in the theatre is a result of group experiences and an external stimulus rather than an existing dramatic text. One characteristic of devised work is that it is multi-layered and often uses multi-media, drawing upon various artistic traditions and performance vocabularies. Alison Oddey explains that:

> Devised theatre can start from anything. It is determined and defined by a group of people who set up an initial framework or structure to explore and experiment with ideas, images, concepts, themes or specific stimuli that might include music, text, objects, paintings or movement. A devised theatrical performance originates with the group while making the performance, rather than starting from a play text that someone else has written to be interpreted.
>
> (Oddey, 1994, 1)

It was with Théâtre Repère that Lepage learned how to further develop his devising skills and to use *The RSVP Cycles.* In performance-writing, his main focus was on the interaction between the actor, the space and the objects, and also how to use the actor's personal material as a resource from which to create scenes. Above all, *The RSVP Cycles* taught Lepage how to make his own material relevant and to place his subjectivity at the centre of a creative process. He places importance on intuition, accidental discovery and a group's collective unconsciousness to generate the work points to a very personal nature of creative process. As with any other devising process, Lepage creates performance from a group's unconsciousness, approaching collective material as a vast chaotic source of creativity, where the artist shapes and translates images into experiences that can be communicated to the audience.

Circulations went on a national tour, and at the La Quinzaine Internationale de Théâtre du Québec it won the Grand Prix, awarded for the best Canadian production. This recognition effectively placed Théâtre Repère on the national map of promising collective companies. *Circulations* pointed to Lepage's directing style which was founded on a collage of languages and diverse places, taking the story through different geographical locations. This was followed by the collectively devised *The Dragons' Trilogy*, in which Lepage acted and directed (Figures 1.1 and 1.2). Through an extensive world tour, this was the production which established Lepage's international reputation. Before *The Dragons' Trilogy* he was known as a member of Théâtre Repère – after the international success of the production, Repère was known as Robert Lepage's group. Lepage's directing was favourably received by critics, and he was seen as someone who had managed to build 'a bridge between the world of visual, physical avant-garde theatre, post-Pina Bausch, and the ancient tradition of the saga or epic storytelling' (Hemming, 1991, 5). The success of *The Dragons' Trilogy* in London's Riverside Studios in 1989 marks Lepage's entry into the milieu of international contemporary intercultural theatre, and comparison of his theatrical language to that of Peter Brook.

Lepage's emphasis on performance-writing through theatrical elements is similar to what the French director **Roger Planchon** referred to as *écriture scénique* (scenic writing) or **Richard Schechner's** notion of performance text. The emphasis on *mise-en-scène* is not on the fixed narrative and character but on the development of a performance, a new theatrical language. The idea of *écriture scénique* revolves around discussions held in the early 1960s concerning the adaptation and modernization of a classical text to be used in contemporary theatre. The classical text would be 're-written' through stage-writing – *mise-en-scène* – and the director, as an author, would create his own '*écriture scénique*' that would contemporise the text. Planchon believed that *écriture scénique* is on an equal footing with the author's written words (Bradby, 1997, 41).

Figure 1.1 Robert Lepage rehearsing the last six-hour version of *The Dragons' Trilogy* in 1987, for Montreal's Festival de Théátres des Ameriques (FTA). Photo by Claudel Huot.

Figure 1.2 Scene from 'The Red Dragon' (first version), the first of the three Parts of *The Dragons' Trilogy*. The interaction between objects, actors and lighting creates the theatrical space.

Lepage's attraction to a plurality of styles and transformation in theatre comes from his belief that performance is a process, a process of change which, for him, is at the heart of ritual as a pre-theatrical form of expression. The audience witnesses the ritual, the passage from one state of existence into another, and is part of this process of discovery. Lepage extends this principle of transfiguration into the way he creates *mise-en-scène*. In theatre we witness transformation. He explains that he is attracted

> to plays in which the characters are transformed, but also to plays in which the sets are transformed and matter is transcendent. It's incredible to be able to travel through time and place, to infinity, all on a single stage. It's the metamorphosis brought about on stage that makes this kind of travel possible.
>
> (Charest, 1997, 135)

Alongside his work with Théâtre Repère, Lepage developed an independent career as an actor, mainly in his solo performances. In this period he developed a theatrical expression founded on visual images, and a collage of various technologies (namely film and photo projections) with a strong live, actor-centred performance. Indeed, his experience with a combination of multi-media and live improvised performance led him to develop his practice as a solo performer. In 1985 Lepage wrote, directed and acted in his first solo performance *Comment regarder le point de fuite* (*How to look at the moment of escape*), produced by Théâtre Repère and presented at the Implanthéâtre, a small theatre venue in Quebec City. This solo show was the first part of a multi-disciplinary performance, *Point de fuite*, presented as a bill of solo performances.

In 1986 Lepage created his first solo performance, *Vinci*, which drew national and international attention to his talents as both an actor and stage writer. He created mobility of space by interacting with the everyday objects on stage, transforming their meaning for the audience. He won the Best Production of the Year Award for this work from the Association Québécoise des Critiques du Théâtre, and his theatricality was widely discussed in Quebec. Although co-produced by Théâtre Repère, *Vinci* was a solo performance. Lepage wanted to find a wider audience, and so began to think about the theatricality needed for performances which could be toured. The first critical recognition for *Vinci* came from performances given outside of Quebec, an affirmation that there was a larger audience with whom he could communicate. *Vinci* went on to have major national and international tours, winning Lepage his first international award in 1987, the Prix Coup de Pouce at the 'Off' Festival d'Avignon, for the best fringe production.

Solo performances established Lepage's international reputation as an artist. They also pointed to his multi-media *mise-en-scène* through the use of cinematic and photographic images. It was with his second solo show, *Needles and Opium* (1991), that Lepage gained international recognition – particularly for his integration of visual technology into live performance, using film projections as a vital element of the performer's action. The production toured until 1996 (with another actor from 1994, once Lepage had finished developing the performance). This approach to *mise-en-scène*, made up of a collage of forms and media where a live performer was juxtaposed to technology and recorded images, was subsequently developed, particularly in his solo performances, throughout the 1990s.

In 1987 he co-wrote and co-directed *Polygraph* with Marie Brassard, a performer and an initial member of Théâtre Repère, with whom he collaborated on all of his projects throughout the 1990s. The production opened in Quebec City and toured until 1990, going through a continuous process of transformation and development. It was also the first text that was published of his devised performance which was meant to be live without any recording. With *Polygraph* Lepage began to depart from Lessard's live experimental concept of improvised devised scores to the concept of using them as works in progress; cycles that were transformative and eventually led towards a more structured performance text and larger audiences. In 1997 Lepage used the performance text of *Polygraph* as a resource for the development of another cycle using a different medium, that of the cinema, to make the film version of *Polygraph*. In 1989, Lepage and some of the other original members of Théâtre Repère (Marie Brassard, Richard Fréchette and Michel Bernatchez) left Théâtre Repère over artistic differences with Lessard, who wanted to keep Théâtre Repère as an experimental fringe theatre with no presence in mainstream circles. Lepage had, in the meantime, associated himself with mainstream institutional theatres around the world as a freelance director.

In 1988 Lepage received his first commission as a freelance director for a major arts theatre in Montreal, the Théâtre du Nouveau Monde. He staged Shakespeare's *A Midsummer Night's Dream*, setting record audience numbers at the Theatre. A year later, in 1989, he was invited to stage Bertolt Brecht's *Life of Galileo* at the same theatre. Alongside Brecht and **August Strindberg**, Shakespeare is the playwright that Lepage has staged most. In 1989 he collaborated with an English-Canadian theatre company in Saskatchewan on the adaptation of the bilingual project, *Romeo and Juliette in Saskatchewan*. In 1992 he devised the *Shakespeare Cycle*, comprising *Macbeth, The Tempest* and *Coriolanus*, as an international co-production between Quebec, France and Germany. However, Lepage's most significant relationship with a Shakespearean text has been with *A Midsummer Night's Dream*. His interpretation of the text was inspired by **Jan Kott**'s influential book *Shakespeare Our Contemporary*, which offers a highly erotic analysis of *A Midsummer Night's Dream* with hidden sexual subtexts. Lepage's treatment of the text was similar to his approach to devised projects. In a seven-year production cycle, between 1988 and 1995, he directed three different versions of the play, creating three *mise-en-scène*. Each used the previous one as a resource for its own development. Following the first production of *A Midsummer Night's Dream* in the Théâtre du Nouveau Monde, the second phase was in 1992 at the Royal National Theatre in London, and the final version took place in 1995 in Quebec City at the Théâtre du Trident.

Lepage and Théâtre Repère began work on *Tectonic Plates* in 1987. They had originally been commissioned by Lili Zendel, the theatre programmer for the Toronto Harbourfront World Stage Festival, to do a show for the 1988 festival. At the same time they were commissioned to do a collaboration with Glaswegian actors in the Tramway theatre for Glasgow's 1990 European City of Culture celebration. Michael Morris, former artistic director of London's ICA theatre and Lepage's European agent and producer, supported the development and promotion of *Tectonic Plates*. One of the objectives for the company, right from the start of the project, was to experiment with the form and nature of the performance-making process. *Tectonic Plates* extended the method of work previously explored in *The Dragons' Trilogy*; this was developed through phases, on tour, while having set production objectives. It also introduced a new concept – collaboration with actors from different companies who spoke different languages. The idea was to develop the project through cyclical phases until it reached the 'final' phase in Glasgow.

Tectonic Plates was a commission that collaborated with international partners, used the English language, various locations, and had to be developed through different media, from theatre performance to TV and film. In many ways the project pointed to future developments with *Ex Machina*, where Lepage worked with collaborators from other countries, actors speaking other languages, and developed performances that would be transformed into another medium (that of television). Turning theatre performances into film was something Lepage explored further with *The Seven Streams of River Ota*, which became the film *No*, and the filming of his solo show *The Far Side of the Moon* under the same title.

In 1989 Lepage moved to Ottawa, to become the youngest artistic director of the French language section of the Canadian National Arts Centre. This move from the margin towards the centre and institutionalized culture signalled Lepage's own interest in centralizing his activities, and in emulating institutionally supported theatre (the ensemble type of theatre production organization so common in continental Europe). While at the National Arts Centre Lepage continued working on his personal material, creating his second solo show *Needles and Opium*. The performance premiered in October 1991 at the Palais Montcalm in Quebec City, before opening in Ottawa in November at the National Art Centre. *Needles and Opium* became a tribute to the art of Jean Cocteau by using Cocteau's personal life as a resource, including his passion for Raymond Radiguet and his life-long camaraderie with opium. It makes references to Cocteau's aestheticism, quoting his text *Lettres aux Américains*. Lepage's own nostalgia, pain over his own lost love, and the need to look for answers inside one's own artistic heritage were juxtaposed to Cocteau's world. By intertwining the lives and works of Jean Cocteau, Miles Davis and a character called Robert, Lepage's alter ego, *Needles and Opium* explored the contradictions between artistic work and everyday life, and between artistic representation and nature – life itself.

MULTI-DISCIPLINARY PERFORMANCE: *EX MACHINA* (1994–)

In the 1990s Lepage's work was characterized by the mixing of media and digital technology in his theatre and by his involvement with other disciplines, such as opera, film and installations. It was also a period in which Lepage looked for stability, independence and control over all aspects of theatre production. After serving as artistic director at the

National Arts Centre, in 1994 he created his own company in Quebec City, *Ex Machina*, with some of his old collaborators from Théâtre Repère and some new ones (inviting a mixture of artists from opera singers and puppeteers to computer designers and video artists).

Lepage's artistic work in the period with *Ex Machina* has been referred to by critics as the 'Canadian Renaissance' because of his versatile approach to the arts, regularly directing opera and films, mixing media and artistic languages. At this time he made his directorial debut in opera, staging in 1993 for the Canadian Opera Company a double bill of operas – Béla Bartók and Béla Balázs' *Bluebeard's Castle* and Arnold Schoenberg's *Erwartung*. Since then directing opera has become integrated into his multi-disciplinary theatricality, directing in 1999 Hector Berlioz's *The Damnation of Faust*, Lorin Maazel's adaptation of Orwell's *1984* (2005) and Stravinsky's *The Rake's Progress* (2007). In 1993 Lepage directed Peter Gabriel's rock concerts *Secret World Tour* and *Growing Up Live* in 2002. In 1989 he worked as an actor on **Denys Arcand**'s much acclaimed film *Jesus of Montreal*. In the mid-1990s Lepage started working on his first film, *Le Confessional*, which opened in 1995. As a film *auteur* he has made four more feature-length films: *Le Polygraph* (1996), *No* (1998), *Possible Worlds* (2000) and *The Far Side of the Moon* (2003).

In 1993 Lepage collaborated with opera singer Rebecca Blankenship, whom he invited in 1994 to join *Ex Machina* on a new project *The Seven Streams of the River Ota*. Originally titled *Hiroshima Project*, the performance was a commission to mark the 50th year of the nuclear bombing of Hiroshima. The intention was to create a collage from seven different arts, to be split into seven parts, last seven hours and take place in seven locations. The multi-disciplinary project was the inaugural production for *Ex Machina* – as *The Seven Streams of the River Ota* it was internationally launched, together with *Ex Machina,* at the Edinburgh International Festival in 1994. Lepage had visited Japan for the first time in 1993, going to Hiroshima where his guide told him about the city's history and his own experience of the atomic bomb as a *hibakusha* (survivor of the bombing). This personal account made a profound impression on Lepage, and the starting point for the *Hiroshima Project* was the atrocity of the US atomic bombing. Following the pattern set with *Tectonic Plates*, a number of other co-producers from Toronto, Edinburgh, Glasgow, Vienna and Paris marketed the project internationally before it was created.

The intention of the new company was to develop productions through phases in Quebec City and then take them on national and international tours. The process of creation cannot be separated from the social and cultural milieu for which the performance is made, particularly since *Ex Machina* is founded on the idea of international tours and collaborations involving a number of co-producers from different countries performing at international festivals and performance venues. This 'work in progress while touring' approach was fully developed in *The Seven Streams of the River Ota*. It could be said that *Ex Machina*, and later La Caserne (Lepage's specially adapted multi-disciplinary studio), grew out of Lepage's experience with *The Seven Streams of River Ota*. If we look at the space for this performance and the space at La Caserne we can see remarkable similarities. In the production of *Ota* the space is a Japanese house with sliding doors, which hides and is transformed throughout the performance to relate to seven different locations. The studio space in La Caserne consists of a big black box (the studio) at the centre, surrounded on two floors by numerous rooms/small studios which face the central studio. The studio-based black box can be adapted to the travelling needs of this project, which was created through touring world venues.

The choice of name for the company relates to Lepage's artistic interest in hybrid art forms. Apart from the obvious reference to the Ancient Greek drama 'Deus Ex Machina' (god from the machine), that resolves the unsolvable crises of human conditions, the name *Ex Machina* is a central metaphor for the interconnections between the performer and technology, and a meeting place between different arts. Lepage created his most technological and aesthetically elaborate performances with *Ex Machina* – *The Geometry of Miracles* and *The Tempest* 3-D version (1998), *Zulu Time* (1998), a new version of *The Dragons' Trilogy* (2003), *Buskers Opera* and *KA* with Cirque de Soleil (2004) and three solo shows *Elsinore* (1995), *The Far Side of the Moon* (2000) and *The Anderson Project* (2005). Working with hybrid forms combining actors who are simultaneously performers, dancers and musicians with various interdisciplinary artists who bring different skills and techniques into rehearsals is crucial for the development of Lepage's theatricality. This was explored in *The Geometry of Miracles* where he worked with actors as dancers, *Zulu Time* where he worked with digital and robotic artists and *Buskers Opera* where he worked with actors who were singers and musicians. It also embodied the idea of creating theatre and taking it to the audience, instead of bringing the audience to theatre. *Ex Machina* was a global theatre company from the start, not representing any one cultural or national centre but having an international cast along with a network of collaborators and co-producers.

Lepage would not have been able to realize this global, multi-media and cross-cultural theatre if there had not been an investment of 7,000,000 Canadian dollars (approximately £3,300,000) for the creation of La Caserne. This former fire station, on Dalhousie Street in Quebec City, was turned into a multi-media studio by adding modern architectural elements to the existing early twentieth-century design. The new building was a result of collaboration between engineers, architects and stage designers working to create a multi-functional space which was also clearly a production facility. The large black box at the centre of La Caserne is an empty space, similar to a studio theatre but without any fixed arrangements for the audience. Numerous offices, multi-media and digital studios are arranged around the black box space and look into it. Lepage uses this general space for rehearsal, to make sets for theatre productions which are integrated with live performance, as a film studio and also as a live theatre venue. Moving to the new facilities meant that Lepage had a permanent laboratory and a multi-disciplinary creative venue to house his company *Ex Machina*. The intention was to connect with other international centres and to create work that could be taken to international audiences.

The group could now develop the *mise-en-scène* in the relative safety of their production lab before premiering it to international audiences. *The Geometry of Miracles* had a long rehearsal period before opening to the audience, which created problems with co-producers who expected to see a show that was not yet ready. To take the performance on to the next level in cyclical development, Lepage needed to have an open rehearsal in front of an audience. The company realized that for financial as well as artistic reasons their next project, *Zulu Time* (1999), had to confront the audience earlier.

The international partners collaborating on Lepage's productions include, among others, major festivals that create their own networks (such as the Edinburgh International Festival, FTA Montreal, the Festival d'Automne à Paris, Berlin Festspiel and the Sydney Festival) and a number of production partners (for example, Cultural Industry Ltd, London's The Royal National Theatre, London's Barbican Centre and the Brooklyn Academy of Music, New York). With all of Lepage's projects, setting up tours by involving international co-producers (often government-sponsored commissions and theatre festivals) is an integral part of the creative process. Lepage begins working on a project by establishing performance dates and venues before he has devised a production. This serves as an overall frame for the production. Every *Ex Machina* show follows this pattern – international events, festivals, international partners and performing venues have a budget for their themed productions (or commissions), for which Lepage devises a performance. Michel Bernatchez, administrative director of *Ex Machina* and Lepage's North American producer and organizer of new productions, is responsible for pre-arranging his tours.

In order to finance the production process, the international venues and co-producers buy into the project before it is complete. In this way, touring becomes an organic part in the development of the work in progress. It is a well-established practice in the festival network that productions of international theatre companies are commissioned or co-produced, as well as invitations being extended to leading theatre directors such as **Peter Stein**, **Lev Dodin** or **Calixto Bieito**. They form a circuit of internationally sponsored and cultivated theatre, and Lepage as a director became a part of this circuit, with all his productions being co-produced by international partners. However, Lepage works from the actor-audience interaction in a flexible and open performance with continuously changing, unstable structures, which often poses problems for expensive, high-art events that require a finished product. Also, in recent years, the practice of EU governments paying money in advance for large-scale projects has been difficult to maintain, while Lepage's shows are becoming more expensive and harder to fund. The funding of a production is ruled by business logic, either through the state or privately, but co-producers need an assurance that the final cultural 'product' will attract critical recognition and mainstream approval, thus providing publicity as well as profitability for its sponsors.

In recent years Lepage has discovered that the balance between a big production frame and the work-in-progress approach is difficult to maintain. His work process depends on intuition and spontaneous discovery, which is difficult to maintain with financial structures where co-producers need definitive results. In the programme for his fourth solo show, *The Far Side of the Moon*, Lepage explained his approach to *mise-en-scène*:

> I consider myself a stage author, understanding the *mise-en-scène* as a way of writing. For example, in this work, the ideas from the *mise-en-scène* alternate with the actors' lines, one leads to the other … What fascinates me about the act of creation is that you fill a space with objects that have no relation to each other, and because they are there, 'all piled up in the same box', there is a secret logic, a way of organising them. Each piece of the puzzle ends up finding its place.
>
> (Lepage, 2002)

This approach underpins the key concerns of Lepage's performance – the ways in which fragments are related and, ultimately, how the puzzle is composed into a performance. Lepage often compares the rehearsal process to a psychotherapy session (in fact he likes to use a psychotherapy session as a way of telling a story to the audience), where the hidden side of the human personality is allowed to come out in front of someone who is observing them.

Dependence on the global cultural network in order to produce shows resulted in a setback in 2001, when the premier of *Zulu Time* in New York and its subsequent world tour was cancelled. This new version of *Zulu Time* was produced by Lepage's *Ex Machina* and Peter Gabriel's *Real World Ltd.*, and at one million Canadian dollars was considered to be the most expensive Lepage production to date. It was also anticipated that a separate company would be set up to commercially promote and internationally tour *Zulu Time* after its New York launch. The performance was due to take place on 21 September at the Roseland Ballroom, as part of a two-month festival entitled *Quebec New York 2001*. Its open-form technological cabaret structure, which could transform and invite various artists from different places on tour and which could be adapted to the cultural circumstances of specific locations, made *Zulu Time* an ideal project for both artists. However, the events of 11 September 2001 (seemingly prophesied in *Zulu Time* with its Middle Eastern terrorists and the crashing of hijacked airplanes) caused the cancellation of the New York premiere and the subsequent tour. In this case, art preceded life and displayed characters described by one critic as 'human automata, animated objects incapable of anything but the most gross emotions – universal lust, a drug smuggler's greed or a terrorist's hatred' (Radz, 28 June 2002). The events of 11 September 2001 transformed *Zulu Time* and the cultural and social dialogue around it.

CONCLUSION

Lepage has built a considerable international reputation over time, beginning with a small experimental theatre in Quebec City in the early 1980s. Starting off in Quebec's theatre fringe scene, his theatricality being able to communicate with an international audience has made Lepage one of the key theatre practitioners of our time. He has received prestigious awards and numerous recognitions for his artistic creativity over the years. In 1999 he received the medal of l'Ordre National du Québec. In 2002 he was awarded the French Legion of Honour and was the recipient of the Herbert Whittaker Drama Bench Award for his outstanding contribution to Canadian Theatre. In 2003 he was awarded the most prestigious Prix Denise-Pelletier by the Government of Québec for his services to theatre arts.

Lepage's theatre is founded on a non-verbal performance language, which is able to communicate outside the Québécois cultural setting and the francophone linguistic milieu. Lepage's use of a non-verbal theatrical language that brings together physical improvisations, playing with objects, cinematic images and visual projections, can be seen within the context of Québécois cultural politics as an attempt to communicate globally by exporting theatre to international audiences and to express Québécois concerns without the limitations of verbal language. The inability to reach a wider audience outside of Quebec with productions in French language forced Lepage to take his stories to another level, and to replace the centrality of verbal language with total theatre and theatrical language. Because Lepage was unable to find a forum for his work within the traditional text-based theatre forms, either as an actor or director, he had to find a suitable way of expressing himself through scenic writing.

His creative process starts from intuition, and through free associations allows the group of collaborators to look for, and make, poetic connections. Lepage discovered his creative context in collective performance, working simultaneously as an actor and director and devising material by looking into and borrowing from different cultures, media and art forms to express his own position. His theatrical language came out of the need for personal expression, to overcome the limitations of traditional theatre forms and the obstacles of language.

2

WRITINGS ON
THE TECHNIQUES OF
PERFORMANCE CREATION

INTRODUCTION

Robert Lepage's practice can be seen in the tradition of 'director's theatre'. Like **Ariane Mnouchkine**, Peter Brook, **Robert Wilson** and **Elizabeth LeCompte**, Lepage is a director-author of performance. In the course of the twentieth century, the *mise-en-scène* became redefined as an independent artistic element, a vehicle of theatricality rather than simply an extension of the text. The director became author of the *mise-en-scène*, and the *mise-en-scène* a separate artistic expression from the written text. Lepage may start from an existing text, as in William Shakespeare's *A Midsummer Night's Dream* or August Strindberg's *A Dream Play*, but it is ultimately the collective process of discovery through rehearsals, not a pre-defined concept, which determines the performance vision and the outcome.

This chapter analyses the main texts on Lepage's performance practice, contained in a book of interviews first published in French in 1995: *Robert Lepage – Quelques zones de liberté*, by Rémy Charest. The book was translated into English in 1997 as *Robert Lepage – Connecting Flights*, from which most of the quotations and ideas discussed in this chapter are taken. Although this is Lepage's book, where he discusses his own work, he refers to a plural 'we' and to a group work. He very rarely uses the first person when describing the creative process. His discussion of practice is done rather fragmentarily and anecdotally. The text is a loose organization of what are at times very general ideas, quoted from various sources, on theatre, art and life. However, in these interviews Lepage does not talk about his performance technique or how his theatre is actually achieved. He does not give the 'method' behind his creative process. In order to point to Lepage's performance technique and contextualize his practice, this chapter's analysis of the writings will be complemented by my own interviews with Lepage (conducted over the last eight years) and by looking at Lawrence Halprin's seminal book *The RSVP Cycles: Creative Processes in the Human Environment* (1969). However, *Robert Lepage – Connecting Flights* remains the key writing that authors Lepage's voice and from which his essential ideas on technique and approach to theatre practice can be deduced.

EVOLVING THE CREATIVE PROCESS

Any writing about a living author is in danger of undermining the totality of his creative opus, particularly when one is writing about such a prolific author as Lepage, who is simultaneously very active in different media (theatre, film and opera). Lepage turned 50 in 2007, so it can be expected that the next decade of his life will be marked with new and different productions evolving out of his creative process. The analysis in this chapter does not attempt to be exhaustive but to set up some key parameters of Lepage's creative process, as established by his own voice through interviews.

This is the first book to engage with the rehearsal techniques of Lepage's performance practice. The stated purpose at the beginning of the book is to explain Lepage's process of devising and directing. This chapter examines the most important texts on Lepage's theatre practice. However, this is not an easy task. Unlike some other practitioners in this series (Barba, Chekhov and Boal), who are interested in a theoretical and pedagogical approach to their own performance practice, Lepage does not provide any direct or concrete assertions of his methods. He does not write about his own process and does not have his own book dealing with the key elements of his technique and exercises. Lepage is not intellectual or analytical about his own theatre; rather, he sees himself as a practitioner, a 'renaissance' man who is able to do various arts and whose art is inseparable from his way of living. When Lepage does talk about his work in interviews, he talks about his views of theatre and arts, often in a very broad and multi-referenced way, always connecting his theatre to his personality. He points out that his work has followed the direction of his life and that his theatre was shaped by what he always wanted to do – to travel and to know other countries (Charest, 1997, 115).

A number of considerations have informed the choice of *Robert Lepage – Connecting Flights* and *The RSVP Cycles* as the key references for this chapter. The former centres on what Lepage says about his own work and the thematic concerns that resulted from his performance practice. It also gives valuable information on what Lepage considers to be essential in his theatre. On the other hand, the material from *The RSVP Cycles* offers an understanding of a creative method that is at the core of Lepage's practice – transformation of performance through cycles. In a cyclical structure, the opening of a performance to the audience serves as a starting point for devising the next cycle. Undoubtedly Lepage's performance techniques will continue to evolve, but the inspiration and stimuli founded on re-adapting *The RSVP Cycles* to solo and collective creation will remain a dominant aspect of Lepage's practice.

GEOGRAPHY: TRANSFORMATIONS AND CONNECTIONS

In the Introduction to *Robert Lepage – Connecting Flights*, Rémy Charest observes that at the centre of Lepage's theatre is 'something which lies at the very heart of theatre: transformation and connection' (Charest, 1997, 9). Transformation lies at the heart of Lepage's creative process and is the reason behind his elusive and ephemeral theatricality. Lepage wants theatre performance to be fluid, open to change, an association of ideas that connects with the audience. He does not want to start from set goals and pre-defined outcomes; rather, he is interested in discovering goals throughout the rehearsals. In opposition to the obvious synergy in theatre production between playwright, director, designers, actors and technicians, where all the production elements work towards creating an end result that is underpinned by the director's concept, Lepage works towards an unknown destination. Lepage explains that the group does not lead their production project ...

... to a given place. We let the production guide us there. We try not to force our ideas, our concepts, on to it; the show has its own logic, poetry, rhythms, that we have to discover. This is as true for a newly created work as it is for an established play.

(Charest, 1997, 99)

The performance narrative is found and developed through a process of transformation that may take several years of touring in different countries before reaching its final destination. Lepage points out that 'crossing geographic borders is also a way of crossing artistic borders ... ' (Charest, 1997, 29). Indeed, geography has an important place in Lepage's life and work. As an artist he makes work for touring, performances that are presented at international venues and festivals for a global audience, where he constructively encounters different cultures. His theatre is typically done through international co-productions with dozens of festivals and major international venues (Figure 2.1). Moreover, his devising process of developing the performance narrative by targeting international audiences and through international tours is reflected in the narratives themselves. Typically, in his original projects, characters go out into the world to another location in order to find something about themselves. On this journey they establish a connection with something that is missing, something that will help them transform by discovering a truth about themselves. This passage, a journey of self-discovery, always includes a going out of one's original location. In this development, personal geography is inseparable from spatial geography. As Lepage says, his point of view is that of someone who has a strong interest in geography (Charest, 1997, 42).

Lepage explains that in their productions the group attempts to integrate

different places and periods ... telling distinctive stories about these places. When you actually travel, you discover the essence of a country or a city, you perceive what makes it unique, what its soul is made of. In this sense, the shows are travel narratives and their success can perhaps in part be measured in the same way as we measure a trip. We are either travellers or tourists. A successful production communicates a traveller's experience.

(Charest, 1997, 37)

As seen in chapter one, Lepage approaches performance as an open rehearsal rather than a finished production. The audience's interpretation

Figure 2.1 Poster for the second version of *The Dragons' Trilogy*, for the VII Chekhov International Festival in Moscow in July 2007.

helps Lepage and the group to make further transformations and connections between the various parts of the devised material. The performance presented to the audience is 'P'erformance as a final part of *The RSVP Cycles*, and not necessarily a finalized and fixed performance as expected in professional theatre; on the contrary, the performance structure remains fluid and open to further change. The presence of the audience during the performance is used as a stimulus to help the group put in place all the parts that have been explored in rehearsals. This area of 'work in progress' and creative process is what interests Lepage.

Lepage believes that the fact the performance is not finalized when it first opens to the audience is key to the devising process. In fact, he feels the material is only really found through the interaction between audience and actors during the performance. Over time, the material written and researched during the rehearsal period continues to work in the group's sub-consciousness. The audience presence then facilitates the opening up of this material through improvisations and interaction with all the elements from the performers' environment. Lepage creates from intuition, asking his performers to be free to 'write' their text through associations, spontaneous discovery and playing with resources, accepting that meaning comes after the fact. Lepage's devising and directing process understands performances as rehearsals before an audience, where the audience witnesses creativity happening in front of them. Lepage sees the creative process as being inseparable from using a collection of improvised and random, accidental events. He is deliberately inviting chaos and provoking spontaneous reactions in a process that is more similar to children playing than to 'serious' professional acting.

Lepage is attracted to eclecticism and transformation in theatre because they represent change which, for him, is at the heart of rituals as a pre-theatrical form of expression. The passage from one state of existence into another (as in, for example, the transformation of water and bread into the body and blood of Christ) is witnessed by the audience, who become part of this process of transfiguration. First it can be a young actor playing an older character or cross-gender casting. On a second, more spiritual level, the audience come to see transformation when an actor is inhabited by a character or *vice versa*. Finally, transformation is part of the narrative when, through the text, characters are faced with obstacles that cause them to undergo change and to metamorphose through the play. Lepage, as we have seen in chapter one, is attracted to theatre where metamorphoses occur throughout the journey of a play – of character and space alike.

In Lepage's *écriture scénique* the subjective presentation of one performer is contextualized through the use of various media and the collective interpretation of a group. It is the use of objects that defines its meaning for the observer. For example, in a Lepage production a row of chairs can become trees if put one on top of the other (as in the 1992 London version of *A Midsummer Night's Dream*) or indicate an aeroplane when an actor lies stomach-down on them with his arms extended sideways (as in the first version of *The Dragons' Trilogy*). It is through the actors' interaction with objects that the new meaning is created. Theatre space comes out of actors' actions that has to reflect their personal material and experience. This can be seen in *The Seven*

Streams of the River Ota via the simultaneous action of various characters in the bathroom engaged in their own events as if they were alone in the space; or in *Tectonic Plates* where stacks of books initially represent a library, but with different lights and projection onto a pool of water create an illusion of a New York apartment block. The process of transformation is not something that is explained to the audience, as an exciting trick, but rather it is something that is experienced by them as part of the performers' storytelling.

COMBINING ARTS AND CULTURES

References to Asian culture in theatre, music and dance are relevant to Lepage's performance practice. Although he has not been to China, Lepage and the other co-creators of *The Dragons' Trilogy* rely heavily on their 'knowledge' of China (Figure 2.2). He is particularly influenced by Zen Buddhism. However, Lepage plays on duality of position – to local culture his position is that of an outsider, while to international cultures it is of a local Quebecker character. He has a tourist's fascination with other cultures, represented in his productions by a local Quebecker character who tries to engage with the outside world and in this process finds out something about himself and his past.

Lepage's version of intercultural theatre allows him freedom to use various cultural and artistic resources as a material for his devising.

Working with such a plurality of media, traditions, styles and artistic forms potentially re-frames the role of director as a facilitator for collective creativity. By bringing together multiple perspectives, Lepage is outlining a new understanding of the director's role and the creative approach to performance-making. Lepage's performances combine personal and collective perspectives and multiple points of view, typically connecting and confronting different cultures. The transformation of forms that characterizes Lepage's performances comes out of the connections between these different cultures. His description of a Sunday afternoon in a park in Tokyo, where an open-air concert brought together all kinds of rock groups to perform, is very telling about his own appropriation of intercultural performance:

> You see Elvises, Marilyn Monroes, Led Zeppelins etc. But they filter the music in a very different way from us. Our Elvis impersonators do everything they can to reproduce the King, but they do it less well than he did. So they do Elvis

Figure 2.2 Scene from 'The White Dragon' (first version), the third of the three Parts of *The Dragons' Trilogy*. Pierre (Robert Lepage) and the third Yukali (Marie Brassard) are in Pierre's studio with a light installation resembling a constellation and Chinese yin and yang symbols. Photo by Claudel Huot.

Japanese-style, giving him a specifically Japanese character. They don't imitate the West. They seem to transcend it.

These games of superimposition create a kind of 'pizza' style of working ...
They have no problem performing the role of a samurai to the music of
Brahms or mixing very disparate techniques in the same show.

(Charest, 1997, 45–6)

Lepage's free interpretation and 'borrowing' from other cultural
resources (art forms, objects, texts, music, etc.) appropriates any
emotional or material content that can become the starting resource
for a performance. Lepage observes that, 'There is the physical place and
then there's what the place represents for you. The China of the *Trilogy*
was a China that suited what we wanted to say in the production'
(Charest, 1997, 35). His intercultural transposition subverts the original cultural and social context found in a location, or the art forms
of the tradition which he is using as a stimulus for devising, to a newly
found meaning established within the performance's context. As in
performance art, his performances eclectically connect varied artistic
forms from the Japanese theatre traditions of **Noh** and **Bunraku** to
Kaprow's 'happenings' and **installation art**. Any artistic form can
become material for improvisation and playing, and anything is possible if it is justified by the actors' actions. For example, in *The Dragons'*
Trilogy Occidental actors are openly playing Oriental characters; in
The Seven Streams of the River Ota traditional Asian art forms are
directly quoted as part of the *mise-en-scène*.

Oriental references, particularly Japanese, were not only important
to Lepage as stimuli for devising, but also for the development of his
style of intercultural theatre. His fascination with the East helped him
understand the West, and more importantly himself. He believes that
the East gave him a mirror to see himself in. 'How can you understand the
West, the culture of the twentieth century, when you're a Quebecker
with virtually no cultural means at your disposal to interpret the
world?' (Charest, 1997, 36). He extends the special and geographical
circumstances that characterize Japan and Canada to a metaphor for
cultural difference and human behaviour. Lepage says: 'The Japanese
live in apartments the size of handkerchiefs, which means that they have
had to create a considerable interior space, an infinite one. In Canada,
space is available in a very concrete and obvious way; we have the
potential to develop an interior space, but tend not to because of our

conditioning, because of our perception of space' (Charest, 1997, 43). This approach to inner space can be seen in the actor's performance in traditional Japanese theatre *Noh* or dance *Butoh*, which is ruled by 'an inner vocabulary' – where a large inner space occupies a very small outer space – which is very codified and precise. As he observes, only enough is disclosed to allow the audience to imagine an inner poetic landscape. He points out that:

> Those who have mastered this [*Butoh*] discipline have learned to develop a series of inner images ... waterfalls in their knees, floating clouds in their arms, and so on. The dancer creates an extremely compact universe. The richer and more colourful this universe, the bigger this poetic landscape, the better the movement. As a result, both in *Butoh* and in theatre, their passion is mostly an inner one. What you see on the outside is always infinitely subtle. You see the trace of an emotion, never the emotion itself.
>
> (Charest, 1997, 43)

The lack of space also creates cultural transparency, where different ideas are put together but are still visible in their original form. Lepage continues: 'The density of the Japanese culture is so great they have no difficulty inserting other cultures into their own, like a sheet of paper slipped into a pile' (Charest, 1997, 45). This over-layering of cultures is the result of transformation and connection in Lepage's theatre. He finds the essence of a play by constantly re-working and changing the found images. In this process, Lepage and the group insert new images (stimuli) into existing material in such a way that the old ideas are still present and continue to affect the new outcomes.

THE CYCLES

In every one of Lepage's devised projects, journeys are central to the development of the action and the story plot. The transformations and connections that come out of the characters' journeys are actually an outcome of the work method. This is a way of devising that is relevant to *The RSVP Cycles* and in the process of cyclical change. Lepage does not talk directly about his directing and devising techniques, since he sees himself as facilitator and editor, and he only makes occasional references to *The RSVP Cycles*. However, his performance practice, regardless of the media he uses to express himself (theatre, film, opera or installation), is based on a creative process that is rooted in, and developed out of, the work of American dance-theatre visionary practitioner Anna Halprin. The transformation of Lepage's performance narrative occurs because of the use of *The RSVP Cycles*, which are based on a cyclical structure that is concerned with process rather than with product (Figure 2.3). Lepage summarizes the creative value of *The RSVP Cycles* as an innovative, non-linear method of working:

> In the writing process, there also is a peripheral listening: the sets are designed at the same time that the lines are improvised, that the characters are defined, that the costumes are cut or chosen, that the lighting is conceived. We don't follow the normal production process, setting the text first and the lighting instruments last. Since *En Attendant*, the first show I did using *The RSVP Cycles*, I have worked this way: all is knitted together from the beginning.
>
> (Lefebvre, 1987, 33)

This section will use *The RSVP Cycles* to examine how Lepage relates and talks about his practice. As seen in chapter one, the initials RSVP stand for Resource, Score, Valuation and Performance – arranged in

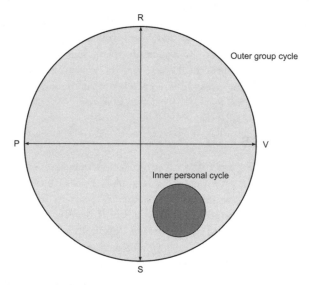

Figure 2.3 *The RSVP Cycles* diagram.

the convenient order RSVP as an invitation to the audience to respond. The most important value of *The RSVP Cycles* for Lepage is that they can be adapted to any human creative process and can have a varied range of applications, from increasing personal creativity to being used in psychotherapy. This flexibility suits Lepage's working process.

Fundamentally, *The RSVP Cycles* are a process of becoming; they pose questions relevant to the creation process – how does it function, what energizes it, how does it influence human action in all fields of art? Resources (R) are the emotional and physical material that performers use to create from. The scores (S) are at the centre of *The RSVP Cycles*. Lawrence Halprin, Anna's husband, started to form his theory by presuming that the creative process is visible through scores as a recording of a process. Using the example of musical scores, Halprin extended the meaning of the term to include all human endeavours. He defines scores as 'symbolization of processes which extend over time' (Halprin, 1969, 1). The term 'Valuaction' (V) joins two words to suggest looking for a value in the action. Valuaction is not about evaluation, which is a psychological process, but about selecting the best from a number of improvised scores so that it can be developed further into a performance. Although Lepage and more established members would have more input, Valuaction is the collective decision-making process of the cycle. 'Performance' (P) refers to improvisations of these selected scores and 'is the "style" of the processes' (Halprin, 1969, 2). This way of creating is about the process of discovery through improvisation rather than rehearsing for a final product.

Lawrence Halprin wrote that, 'it is through them [scores] that we can involve ourselves creatively in "doing", from which, in fact, structure emerges – the form of anything is latent in the process' (1969, 5). However, the scores are a system of notation but are not a closed coding of an art work, as are the stage directions in a play or the director's book with annotated *mise-en-scène*. The scores are, rather, vehicles for the continuous transformation of the material. Halprin explains that the scores function through processes, exploration, chance, openness, emotional states and irrationality (1969, 192–95). These qualities of the scores, and in particular the fact that they are cyclical and in process, are the building blocks of Lepage's transformative *mise-en-scène*. Out of these initial ideas, it is clear to what extent Lepage's own artistic concepts are influenced by the RSVP scores – most importantly, structure is discovered through the process embodied in the scores and arising out of chance and intuition.

In 1982, when Lepage became a member of Théâtre Repère, he brought with him the improvisational skills and approach to performance that he had learned from Alain Knapp, which were based on the actor-author's intuition. Lepage learned how to use *The RSVP Cycles* from Lessard's *Repère Cycles*. For Lepage, it is important for *The RSVP Cycles* to represent something quite different for each deviser individually and to produce different results in performance. The influence of *The RSVP Cycles* on Lepage's directing and devising can be seen in the non-linear and fragmented nature of his storytelling, as well as in his way of expressing personal and group collective fantasies, memories and dreams. In devising, the relationship between the personal and the collective is essential. Subjectivity (as an extension of one's own subject self into an outer world) is central to the creative process.

'Repère' as a personal reference point or landmark is very important for Lepage's devising, since his productions are founded on the subjective perception – the own reference point that each performer brings into the work process. Lessard's *Repère Cycles* are best described in the sequence in which they occur. The word 'Repère' is made from the stages of the Cycles: Re – resources, P – partition or score, E – evaluation, Re – representation or performance. Repère demonstrates the effect of reducing the importance of words, and increasing the expressiveness of other theatrical tools (movement, light, sound, objects, etc.). It is a tool that enables actors to relate to various theatrical means as a stimuli for their action.

In Repère theatre practice, which is fundamentally how Lepage understands and talks about *The RSVP Cycles*, (R)esource is a starting point of devising which can be both human and physical. (P)artition (the French for score) is a scene that is improvised through the use of resources. Partition has to open the performer's consciousness to all external impulses, in order to look at the different possibilities for using resources and establishing personal responses that could also be emotionally moving for others. During rehearsals, partition has to liberate the themes of the performance and develop the emotional state. This means that partition has to be separated into two phases – exploration and synthesis. The exploratory period allows freedom to investigate the unsuspected, while the synthesis part of the cycle relates to Valuaction. It is the assessment of created work, deciding which elements should be kept and developed in the performance. Synthesis collects all the elements into an order to help understand the effect of the exploration and to know their direction. Synthesis is the process of defining the creative impulse, a critical viewing of unformed material, consciously creating an artistic entity, a form, based on experimental subconscious self-expression. The selective attitude of the actor-creator is both influenced by the group and by his or her own understanding of their scores created in the exploratory period.

In the 'Re-presentation' part of the cycle, which is a performance of synthesized material, it is the director/outside eye who facilitates the meaning of the performance. This is inevitable due to the very nature of group creation in theatre; someone has to take control within the group for the choices made regarding specific aspects within the performance. As in *The RSVP Cycles*, 'Re-presentation' can be used as a resource for the development of yet another cycle. Usually Lepage calls an open or public rehearsal to present what has been achieved in a cycle to the audience. It is important to have collective feedback at the end of a cycle to allow for progression into another cycle.

For Lepage the essence of *The RSVP Cycles* is the performer's action in front of the audience or someone in the position of an observer. This emphasis on the actor's action and own performance material comes from *The RSVP Cycles*, where everything starts from movement (as the 'idea of body') and then develops into a narration that makes personal sense to the creator. Jacques Lessard explains that the connection between physical action and internal impulse comes from 'a sequence of movements that make you conscious of what is happening inside you' (Beauchamp, 1990, 49). He continues to explain that Anna Halprin made these movements for the spine as the centre that controls all the movements of the body. The movement rituals are similar to Yoga, except that movement flows in a sequence. It is personal movement in the same way as Lepage's actors are authors of their own text and bring their own material that comes out of them.

DISCOVERING HIDDEN STORIES

Lepage's performance practice is particularly interesting because of the dynamism and tensions that exist between collective and individual creativity. Out of this individual-group relation, stories are discovered throughout the work process. Lepage directs a group of actors that conceives performance collectively through improvisations as a group working together over long periods of time. Simultaneously, this creative process is also driven by individual actor-authors who 'write' their character, or often other characters and their action. As facilitator, Lepage defines the balance between group and individual work; however, this relation is also present within the cyclical structure of the work. For each member of the collective creative process there is an outer circle – a group cycle – and a smaller inner circle – an individual cycle. The *mise-en-scène* is, therefore, an outcome of the interaction between the cycles, and of the performers' collective and individual engagement with different themes, ideas and personal references. By being involved in all aspects of performance creation, Lepage facilitates these dynamics. He puts together all the different strands of the collective work process. Therefore, the dynamism of the actors' creative process is essential to generate the material from which he works as a director-author.

The creative process typically begins with group brainstorming sessions, which are often followed by individual drawings of the performer's impressions on the starting resource, and extensive individual improvisations that produce a number of scores. Lepage starts with 'Performance', the last part of the creative cycle, using improvised scenes that he can edit and place in various contexts. 'Performance' becomes the material that will eventually be performed publicly. This provides a new creative impulse that triggers the development of subsequent performance cycles. It is important to emphasize that each member of the group brings their own personal resources. Lepage's process as a director is determined by the individual characteristics of the actor-creator and the collective environment in which the work in progress takes place. Lepage points out that directing is not

> the sole property of the director. With our approach, it comes out of a collective effort. When we rehearse with actors, we discover and uncover the play. When I direct, my approach is closer to that of a student than that of a teacher. I think this is what makes the play continue to evolve right until opening night and even beyond it.
>
> (Charest, 1997, 167)

We need to be aware that in Lepage's devising, the search for the stories takes place throughout the creative process and does not stop on the opening night. In fact, performances are open rehearsals before an audience. Lepage points out that, for the actors, the opening night is usually a culminating point when problems are finally resolved. However, for his group of actors opening night is another kind of discovery, a moment in the evolution of the performance, and often everything can change and be re-structured between dress rehearsal and opening night. In fact, part of the excitement of theatre for Lepage is the possibility of reinventing things each time they are done (Charest, 1997, 106). Discovering stories, adapting them, and finding the best way to express them is, for Lepage, a constant search and struggle throughout the life of the performance. Sometimes the result of the improvisations is good. A discovered scene, movement or image is 'invited to stay' in the further development of a performance. Nevertheless, that invention may be aesthetically strong but with a meaning that remains on the surface, an image that looks good but does not have much substance. Also, it may happen that the found scenes only become alive and relevant for further dramaturgical development once presented to the audience.

Writing performance in front of an audience comes from Alan Knapp's method of work. For Lepage, when this process is pushed far enough, it looks like it has been previously written while it is actually improvised in front of the audience. This improvisation as 'writing' is a crucial aspect of the devising process because, as Lepage explains, stage-writing is like digging, looking for a subject matter that is unknown.

> The main thing that I brought back with me [from Alan Knapp] as an actor or as a stage director is that you have to know how to tell a story, how to write, how to structure. It is important to work with the intelligence of the actors. Very often actors are brought to play the emotions of the story or to play the characters, but they are actually very interesting writers. They are not good writers, but they have their writing ideas as performers. If you believe what Planchon or Alan Knapp say, that directing is writing and stage design is writing, then you also have to consider acting as part of writing.
>
> (Lepage, 1999)

In Lepage's experience the group may, without realising it, find something that relates to the audience and establish an emotional connection with them. Artists do not have control over this aspect of the creative process, where the meaning behind the stories comes out at the end of the creative process instead of at the beginning. However, Lepage expects each actor-author, in a collectively devised performance, to find their own personal mythology. He points out that Picasso saw an artist's task as discovering things and then afterwards finding out what they mean. Lepage supports this point of view, recognizing that there is a huge gap between artistic intentions and results. As in poetry, the actor-creator has to make new expressions and then search for what is hidden behind them. Lepage urges practitioners to accept this, to understand that meaning comes after the fact.

Experimenting in a studio and using the audience as partner and mirror are an important part of discovering the stories and finding the meaning that follows. It is important to show the project to the audience at a certain stage in its development. Lepage notes that, when the audience has not related well to some performances, 'it wasn't because we had nothing to say, but rather because our material hadn't sufficiently taken shape at the time they saw it – it was still at the interim stage; we were still building on it in the lab' (Charest, 1997, 129). Lepage believes that contemporary directors like Peter Brook, Bob Wilson and Peter Sellars find their ideas from working in a studio and experimenting with form before creating the play in a definite way with a major theatre company. He promotes the idea that art needs to be free from constraints of industry and public expectations.

INTUITIONS AND ACCIDENTS

Having no pre-conceived ideas can be liberating for the director and actors. It can set them free from the concepts, existing clichés and demands of defined categories of genre and style. However, Lepage's practice is inherent in the very nature of the human creative process. For Lepage, people traditionally want to control and regulate the performance or, as he puts it poetically, 'tame the theatre. The theatre is something wild, without rules, that they want to prevent from growing naturally, organically. For me, unruliness of this kind feeds my work, like an unexpected rainfall' (Charest, 1997, 88). Lepage's theatre comes out of intuition, from accidental creativity and unpredictability. His work process is very chaotic. Following the unknown and unpredictable in theatre-making is similar to Peter Brook's notion of theatre that is 'making the invisible visible'(Brook, 1992). Lepage plays with the production elements (visual images, sounds, movements, space, objects and technology), with the actors' energy and a 'hidden text' until the invisible is made visible through the performance run, through interaction with spectator or audience.

Brook states that his creative process starts 'with a deep, formless hunch, which is like a smell, a colour, a shadow. I have no structure for doing a play, because I work from that amorphous non-formed feeling, and from that I started preparing' (Brook, 1987, 3). Using a shadow as a starting point could very well be applied to Lepage's work process. To free this energy Lepage believes that chaos, as the generator of creativity, is a necessary part of the rehearsal and performance process. If theatre is only about order and rigour, as Lepage sees it, the outcome will be only about order and rigour. 'But it's out of chaos that the cosmos is born – the order of things, yes, but a living, organic, changing one. This is where true creation lies' (Charest, 1997, 88). Lepage provides an important example for his chaos theory, in opposition to order, as he experienced it while working on *The Seven Streams*:

> The two extreme incarnations of World War II, the atom bomb and the concentration camps, both resulted in utter chaos. The art of war, especially the concentration camps, is composed of strictly organized acts that lead behind immense disorder. This kind of extreme organization – creating lists, for example, of all the works written by Jews in order to destroy them and, in this way, destroy the very idea of Jewish people – this organization is completely contrary to the process of creation that comes out of chaos.
>
> The outcome of this highly organized thing, war, is experienced in chaos, and it embodies the end of many things: the end of a war of life, of belief, of loving, the end of certain forms of society. It's in this sense that the idea of the Hiroshima bomb naturally leads us towards the idea of renewal; the idea of death toward the idea of sensuality and life.
>
> (Charest, 1997, 89–90)

The principle of opposition extends not only to Lepage's approach to devising but also to the way he sees creative processes in other arts. For him the contrasts are essential. Lepage suggests that, in painting, to bring out the yellow one has to use black, and in music when one wants to make a musical theme stand out one uses counterpoint. In theatre plays the same thinking applies: 'If you want to reveal life and the instincts to survive and reproduce, you often have to approach them through death' (Charest, 1997, 91).

In devised theatre, the performance is created from the group's unconscious material. Lepage uses that material as a vast chaotic source of creative potentials. He believes that the stories which are first discovered come as images and fragments from memories, dreams, through accidents, and that, if pursued further, they provide material that helps the actor-creator to individually develop their own truth. Similarly, for Brook, the purpose of the performance is to act as a medium to 'transmit truths which otherwise would remain out of sight. These truths can appear from sources deep inside ourselves or far outside ourselves' (Brook, 1987, 107).

Both Brook's and Lepage's approach to collective creativity favours the unconscious mind, echoing Carl Jung's theories of creativity and the unconscious. Jung recognizes two models of artistic creation – psychological and visionary. He explains that the psychological model 'works with materials drawn from man's conscious life, made of all general human experiences, emotions, events' (Jung, 1966, 90). As such, these experiences are implemented as the raw material that the poet-artist clarifies and transfigures. The difference between this and the visionary mode is that the latter derives from primordial experiences, dreams, the unknown depths of the human soul, 'from the hinterland of the human mind, as if it had emerged from the abyss of pre-human ages, or from a superhuman world of contrasting light and darkness' (Jung, 1966, 90). It is evident that Lepage's creative process is not an outcome of the psychological model that comes from the conscious mind, but that it relies on spontaneous discovery, pointing to Jung's visionary mode.

DRAMATURGICAL DEVICES

A dramaturgical tool in connecting discovered scenes and images is Lepage's alter-ego character, Pierre Lamontagne. Pierre is a linking character, a vehicle that propels events in a story. As Lepage explains, he is an all-purpose character who is young and an artist,

> which allows us to place him almost anywhere, in almost any circumstances. He's a very flexible, very mobile character – a blank character, in a way. He provides the link between the story and the audience. His naïve approach towards the events he encounters reflects the spectator's position.
>
> (Charest, 1997, 34)

Important dramaturgical devices that Lepage often uses are dreams and hallucinations (drugs). These alternative states help justify the transitions between different scores (scenes) as movement through time and space, that are thematically connected but are not linked in a cause-effect narrative structure. Critics often pointed out that Lepage's theatricality aesthetically functions as if in a dream. As happens in dreams, reality and fantasy, past and present, collide and transform one into another. In Lepage's performance, events relate to each other in the space without necessarily having a direct cause-effect link. As in a dream structure, the conventional plot is replaced with connection based on association, illusion, metaphor and imagination. Lepage's production of August Strindberg's *A Dream Play* at the Kungligs Dramatska Teatern in Stockholm in 1994 set the scene in a rotating cubicle, where 'time and place do not exist' (Strindberg, preface, 1901). In effect, Lepage's theatricality often subjects the audience to striking and strange imagery, as if in a collective dream.

The use of drugs occupies an important place in almost all of Lepage's original projects, particularly in *Circulations*, *The Dragons' Trilogy*, *Tectonic Plates*, *Needles and Opium*, *The Seven Streams* and *Zulu Time*. Transfiguration often occurs after the characters use drugs. Indeed, drugs are one of Lepage's favourite storytelling devices since they can provide drama-turgical justification for characters that reach out for hidden worlds, and show to us what is behind a scene when the meanings are not readily available or visible at first glance. The performance is devised by the actors themselves by connecting a set of scores (usually events and images) that are independent from each other and have their own structure. The connection between these scores uses external devices that help the introspective process. Not only drugs, but also memories, deaths and journeys are used to create the link between various scores. Like Brook, Lepage believes that finding out the hidden stories is not the result of conscious constructs and the intellectual and psychological understanding of the narrative or characters, but that it grows out of the performer, from their whole body, and the unconscious from which actors can draw material.

Lepage uses **numerology**, exploring numbers and what they represent symbolically in religion, philosophy and mathematics, to discover a hidden structure and find connections between the materials. He uses numerology to establish the connection between number and names or objects that helps in finding hidden meanings. The number seven, which emerged as a key structural device in *The Seven Streams*, is the number of spirituality and harmony. It represents a connection between sprit and body. Lepage points out that this number consists of four plus three, four representing harmony and three spirituality. In numerology, the number that corresponds to Lepage's name is seven. Each letter has a numeric value (A = 1, B = 2, C = 3, etc.) and the sum of each letter in the alphabet totals 61, 6+1 = 7. Each number has a symbol and interpretation that is used for dramaturgical development. These numbers can also be translated into geometrical shapes – a triangle, a square or a cube – that represent human invention and the way humans organize the world and structure the space. There is always a significant number in Lepage's productions – three in *The Dragons' Trilogy*, four in *Vinci*, two in *The Confessional* and *The Far Side of the Moon*.

Throughout the process of discovering the unknown, Lepage, as the director, does not impose his concepts on any overall group decision. He and the group are free to look for emerging meanings that will become the essence of the main narrative of the production. Being a 'facilitator' between the performers and the subject matter and selected starting resources allows Lepage to be at the same time on the inside and the outside of the creative process. Theatre is, as he explains, infinitely greater than we are, because everything is larger than us. Improvising around starting resources leads the group down different paths. Sometimes it is a very small action or a simple image that the group has to look at in order to uncover its meaning and create the order in which the scenes will be played. In this work process, some scenes become a microcosm of the performance. Lepage uses the word 'hologram' to think metaphorically about a dramaturgical 'particle', where one scene in a stage space embodies information for the whole performance, as a particle does in quantum theories. Finding the hologram of the performance is done not by imposing Lepage's personal world on the performers, or his director's vision, but rather by creating environments in which the performers can discover what is hidden from the conscious mind and find the essence of the future performance.

MULTI-MEDIA AND PERFORMANCE ART

Lepage's plurality of vision, which once was considered to be his inability to focus on one thing, is his personal ability to work across different disciplines. Not only is he recognized as a theatre author of multi-media performance, but also he has achieved national and international acclaim as a film director-author with, as mentioned in chapter one, *Le Confessional* (1995), *Polygraph* (1996), *No* (1998), *Possible Worlds* (2000) and *The Far Side of the Moon* (2003). He also directs opera, installations and rock concerts. He is an accomplished performer, writer and designer. In a renaissance way, Lepage is a multi-faceted artist who brings other art forms into his theatre. In a **new baroque** way, this inevitably results in the creation of a collage of references and stimuli combined with an interdisciplinary *mise-en-scène*.

Lepage's theatre is fundamentally about finding ways to tell story to an audience that does not understand your language. It is a performance where narration comes out of personal experience and the use of new and traditional art forms and media, through live and projected images and a combination of different cultures. Lepage is aware that it is very difficult to write and describe production elements such as sound, images and the collective energy of the play. Only once the cycle is completed and the group comes to a certain level of discovery is there a sense of closure, when Lepage eventually records the performance. This is done in order for the members not to forget what was created, since the time-span between rehearsal phases can be six or more months. Also, group members can come and go out of the project and it is important for new members to have access to the recorded process. Once the narrative is fully discovered, the story can cross into another medium – either as a published text as with *Polygraph*, *The Seven Stream of the River Ota* and *The Dragons' Trilogy*, as film for the big screen (*Polygraph*, *No and Far Side of the Moon*) or as TV film (*Tectonic Plates*).

Instead of verbal language, Lepage's performances use different media and technology as the language of theatre. The purpose of technology for Lepage is to serve as a unifying factor to tell stories that bring people together. Lepage compares technology – visual image and light – to fire in its ability to bring people together:

> In the great black of the night, we gather around the fire to tell each other stories. Fire is used to inaugurate important events: the Olympic Games are opened with the lightening of a torch, which, however, does not illuminate the whole stadium. Fire is the symbol of gathering. When we assemble in a cinema and are plunged in darkness the light is restricted to the screen. It's like watching a fire, a light whose shapes and colours are in constant motion.
>
> (Charest, 1997, 124)

The storytelling is done through various artistic forms. It is also important to emphasize that Lepage considers form to be content – form is the vehicle for telling stories. This is similar to the tradition of epic narratives. From Lepage's perspective, theatre is wrongly considered to be a place for words, to belong to the world of literature, where performance starts with a text. He constantly returns to the idea that the theatre is a meeting place for different arts; a place where architecture, music, dance, literature, acrobatics and theatre interact. Lepage insists that this interaction interests him the most, gathering artists together and combining different artistic styles and disciplines.

Perceived like this, Lepage's performance practice may be seen within the tradition of **Richard Wagner**'s concept of *gesamtkunstwerk* (uniting all operatic devices) and **Adolph Appia**'s concept of **total theatre**. At the turn of the twentieth century Appia elaborated on this idea – seeing theatre as an art that could bring together other art forms. According to Appia, dramatic art is defined through three factors: text (music or speech), stage settings (sculptures or painting), and theatre (architecture). He established that movement is the common denominator between the factors that embody various forms of art in theatre (poetry, painting, sculpturing, architecture and music). The aptitude of theatre to include different arts, as indicated by Appia, was also important for other art forms (poetry, music, painting, sculpture). In the twentieth century various art forms found, in the immediacy of theatre performance, a platform to respond to the world's events and deliver their manifestos. This meant that theatre as a medium became a meeting place where different arts could interact. This collage of various arts has been defined as live or performance art, which over time became an art form in its own right. Performance art became a permissive form of expression for personal stories, political ideas and new artistic styles that challenged the old ones. It can be said that Lepage's eclectic theatre is a bridge between performance art and traditional theatre.

'New theatre' in the early 1980s, as defined by US performance art historian Rose Lee Goldberg, included all media and used dance or sound to round out an idea or to refer to film in the middle of a text (Goldberg, 1999). She defines this as 'performance-theatre'. This is a useful term for Lepage's collective and multi-media theatre. Collective creation or devised theatre can also be seen as a way of working that can produce performance-theatre. The emphasis on a moment, an open structure, the ability to change, subjectivity and plurality are all important elements of devised theatre and performance art. The collective creation, as an alternative to a traditional theatre of the cultural 'centre', is free to tell stories that are not part of that 'centre' through means which are borrowed from other arts, cultures and traditions. Like performance art, devised theatre uses vocabulary from dance, music, visual arts, mass media and new technology to introduce them into its own expression. This plurality of styles also has to do with being able to find alternative audiences outside of the mainstream, and relating to their sensibilities not only in content (what the story is about) but in the way it is communicated (how is it told).

The flexibility of Lepage's collective creation to use different forms could be seen within the context of Goldberg's 'performance-theatre'. Some of the key characteristics of performance-theatre are:

- non-text based and event-driven action
- dependency on specific space/location and time, which structures performed events
- subjectivity and an autobiographical approach
- non-conceptual
- absence of pre-conceived ideas
- independence (they are single events created as improvisation and through accidents)
- communication with the audience through a plurality of media, regardless of the audience's verbal language
- the inclusion of the audience in the creative process.

Inviting a variety of forms and styles and communicating through different media also means that performance-theatre is more open and flexible to include personal or group experiences. Like Jean Cocteau, Lepage freely explores on-stage poetic, mythological and aesthetic provocations taken from other sources that have strong subjective meanings. Through Cocteau's poetic work, Lepage was exposed to Dadaist and Surrealist ideas about performance as a spontaneous act and playful event, and art as a highly subjective response to the world. Dada soirées were interactive and improvisational, being directed at the same time as they were performed and including the audience's reaction as part of their development. There were no pre-conceived ideas or scripts to follow, nor did rehearsals seek to create a unified and aesthetically sound production, yet the form was essential as a way of finding a means to express their vision.

It was not until *Needles and Opium*, Lepage's second solo show in 1991, that he experimented with the visuals of *mise-en-scène* achieved through the projections of a 16mm film. The idea was to create an experience that was more than the sum of its parts by including several different forms of representation in one context of performance. For Lepage this reflects contemporary life, which increasingly consists of a plurality of stimuli themed around an apparent absence of destination. Such non-places as shopping malls, airports, lobbies in international chain hotels, fast-food restaurants and holiday resorts, among others, are locations of sameness which are dislocated from the real in a similar way as media 'reality' is through satellite TV and the internet (Augé, 1995). The urban cosmopolitan audience of Lepage's performances readily recognize this context of multiple referencing, (mis)communications, travel, mobile phones and internet, as well as the search for one's own self in other cultures. In his productions, the characters find them- selves in these multiple worlds of mediated experiences and recognize the fractured plurality of their own existence.

Indeed, Lepage's performance practice invokes a plurality of artistic and cultural references through all available resources, juxtaposing live actors with visual images, interlinking technology and live perfor- mance. For example, in *Zulu Time* different art forms were brought together because the technologies were compatible. Particularly since the inception of his production company *Ex Machina*, Lepage's per- formance has been seen as an extension of the actors' action combined with technology. This approach to *mise-en-scène* ultimately creates a collage of man and machine.

LANGUAGES OF A NEW TECHNOLOGY

Although his aestheticism may sound complex, Lepage's performance actually comes out of quite simple means and creates something which is visually exciting and emotionally relevant. He creates performance through all available resources. This was done originally out of the need to use whatever was available for a low-budget production; necessity rather than specific artistic vision. Lepage considers that his production director and long-term collaborator Michel Bernatchez has always been able to define and shape the technical aspects of his projects, focusing on the artistic content and making sure that the artistic and technical aspects develop together (Charest, 1997, 108). Touring a performance has an important role in this developmental process. Touring serves to filter what can stay and what needs to be eliminated, it requires the technical aspects to be simplified. Lepage uses transportable settings made of overhead projections and transparencies, 16mm film, photography, and live and recorded sound. In this way his theatricality is not different from hundreds of small groups working on the fringes in alternative spaces or in universities, where the theatre space includes various technologies to help create the visual images.

From the beginning of Lepage's career, his performances have been described as cinematic and informed by vivid visual images. It is true that cinematography is a powerful inspiration on Lepage's theatricality. On the other hand, commentators on Lepage's film work always use his theatre as a point of critical comparison. However, Lepage does not 'belong' fully to any one media. Because he is also a film director, Lepage's work casts light on a particular interdisciplinary creative process. This process consists of the crossover between theatre as live and film as a recorded art form. Fundamentally, Lepage's approach to the theatre space is to use the stage frame as a film frame. For example, the theatrical space for *Coriolanus* as part of the *Shakespeare Cycle* was framed in a TV screen/antique frieze, and *La Casa Azul* was played behind a transparent film/computer screen.

Bringing different media and technology into the performance is as much an outcome of the rehearsal process as it is an input from the audience. For Lepage:

> the audience that comes to see the theatre today does not have the same narrative education as people 20–30 years ago. If I play in front of an audience in a traditional theatre, the people who are in the room have seen a lot of films, they've seen a lot of television, they've seen rock videos, and they are on the net. They are used to having people telling stories to them in all sorts of ways. They know what different points of view there are. They know what a flash-forward is, what a jump-cut is. If you look at the commercials today, there is no continuity but people have extraordinary acrobatic minds. I think that you have to use that in performance and the shifting of perception is part of that.

You know that the audience is used to having their perception changed by television all the time.

(Lepage, 1999)

Although his productions have all the characteristics of world theatre, with global references reflecting communal themes and concerns, playing for international and cosmopolitan audiences, they are fundamentally local stories with their authenticity coming from home-grown Québécois culture and personal experience. The creative processes work best while working on the material they are more familiar with.

CONCLUSION

Throughout *Robert Lepage – Connecting Flights*, Lepage is presented as a director-author who is characterized by the continuous transformations and connections he makes during the rehearsals and performance run, often changing and discovering stories from one performance/rehearsal to another, from one audience's cultural context to the next. As Lepage observes, working in other countries demands adjustment to the new realities. The principal challenge of working internationally is to be able to compare methods, compare visions of the world, and find a common path that will lead him and the group where they want to go.

Travelling is an important way for Lepage to do theatre, not only because his theatre is about movement through cultures, but because his name has been made through his participation at major international venues and festivals (London, Edinburgh, Avignon, Paris, Tokyo). Yet the dynamism in his performance comes out of a small-scale and inexpensive production frame that is, fundamentally, a 'poor theatre', like the theatre of an alternative group working on the fringe. Lepage's theatre is an elaboration of a small frame, of the aestheticism of the fringe that is projected and expanded onto the larger frame of mainstream international artistic theatre. The tension between the international theatre frame and the aestheticism of the fringe theatre is at the core of Lepage's theatre.

The plurality of readings of Lepage's performance narrative emerges from the collective engagements, as much as from the influences of other cultures. Found narratives are the outcomes of other collaborators and the audience alike. His theatre is not one based on a singular vision, clear aestheticism or an interpretation of grand narratives, but on a multi-layered and polyvalent theatrical vocabulary where theatre performance is an outcome of the totality of theatrical expression. It uses performance text rather than written text – an equal mixture of actor, design, space, visual and audio images, projections and audience – to create the total theatre.

3

PERFORMANCE TEXT: *THE DRAGONS' TRILOGY*

INTRODUCTION

The focus of this chapter is on the devised performance, *The Dragons' Trilogy*. To analyse one performance as a key representative of Lepage's practice, from such a rich range of creative work, could be limiting. However, this is the one production that brings together pre-rehearsal training, creative processes and a collage of art forms and media connecting Lepage's work from the 1980s to his current work. It was performed in two versions, bridging more then two decades of Lepage's work. The first version was developed through cycles between 1985 and 1987, while Lepage was still a member of Théâtre Repère. By the time the second version (with *Ex Machina*) was developed in 2003, Lepage was a well-known international director of theatre, film and opera, as well as being recognized as a solo performance artist. The second version took the previous *Trilogy*, as a resource to create another cycle, and became a published play text in 2005. *The Dragons' Trilogy* is the longest running of Lepage's original productions.

Lepage's directing trademark developed in *Circulations* and his one-man show *Vinci*, but it matured fully through the development of the three phases of *The Dragons' Trilogy*. Evolving from a ninety-minute production into a three-hour performance, *The Dragons' Trilogy* finally became a six-hour performance. The original six-hour version was presented for the first time on 6 June 1987 in Hangar 9, at the 12th Festival de Théâtres des Ameriques (FTA) in Montreal. It won the best show award and gave Lepage his first major recognition as a director. This final cycle produced a performance that became fixed and on tour until 1991. It won a number of prestigious theatre awards, and critics started to contextualize Lepage's theatricality within the tradition of Peter Brook's work. In addition, the production method that it set up was later followed by Lepage in other major epic, interdisciplinary and intercultural projects such as *The Seven Streams of the River Ota, Geometry of Miracles*, *Zulu Time*, and *Lipsynch*. The second version was re-created for the same festival, FTA, in 2003 and was on international tour until 2007. Arguably, Lepage's directing and devising of *The Dragons' Trilogy* remains his most remarkable and longest running theatre work to date, communicating with audiences in the late 1980s as powerfully as with a whole new generation more than twenty years later.

As we saw in chapter two, Lepage's creative process develops through transformation of performance text. This transformation takes place over a period of time through international tours, where the performance evolves in front of an audience. To reiterate, the audience is another partner in the creative process and their response is vital for the development of a performance text. Lepage's theatricality is similar to live performance art events that directly communicate with the audience through actors' improvisations and which have a flexible structure that does not have to be replicated from one performance to the next. However, Lepage's productions are theatre plays and, as such, ultimately aim to discover a structure that will eventually become permanent. In the course of the following chapter, we will analyse the cyclical creative process and devising techniques behind *The Dragons' Trilogy*.

SYNOPSIS OF *THE DRAGONS' TRILOGY*

There are two published recordings of this production. One is the publication of the full performance text (2005), based on the 2003 re-staging of the second version. The other is an account of the 1987 six-hour first version, which appeared in a special issue of the Quebecker theatre journal *Jeu* (1987) that was dedicated to the reconstruction of *The Dragons' Trilogy*. *Jeu*'s account offered a synopsis of the performance, alongside a collection of critical essays and personal accounts of the performance. However, these materials were secondary sources, and it was very hard to establish a personal experience with the performance through them. Although the five-hour second version is strongly founded in the previous 1987 cycle, there are differences between the first (1987) and second (2003) versions of the performance; however, we will not engage with an analysis of these differences and what affected the selection process. Lepage's work is cyclical and is bound to change and develop. Our approach will be to look at how Lepage created this landmark performance and at the techniques he employed. We will be looking at the second version as an example, bringing in elements from the 1987 performance only where differences are important to understand Lepage's performance practice.

To start our journey into *The Dragons' Trilogy*, it is important to understand that the performance text we will use here was not pre-conceived and written as a dramatic text, nor was it ever intended to become a published text. The 2005 published second version is based on a collectively devised theatre that initially developed over three years, and is more similar to ephemeral performance art and multi-media events than to an enduring traditional drama text. This is not a literary text but a per-formance, where visual qualities of images and *mise-en-scène* are more important than words (language) and narrative plot in establishing the meaning of a specific scene. It is important to note that the published per-formance text equally uses French and English, also mixing in Chinese (Cantonese) and Japanese depending on the characters and action on stage.

Lepage recalled that the group wanted 'to do a show about Chinatown and I wanted it to be a trilogy: three parts, three places and three times. Those were my bounds; I had the intuition it was going to lead us somewhere' (Lefebvre, 1987, 33). The initial idea to do *The Dragons' Trilogy* came out of touring *Circulations* in Quebec City, Toronto and Vancouver, where the audience and theatrical community were very responsive. This was why the group wanted to set up the show in these three cities and create a specific performance for each one of them. The starting idea was to create a group of solo perfor-mances with seven actors, organized around the same theme and space, with the performance developing as a site-specific event in each location, communicating with communities across Canada.

The Dragons' Trilogy is a collective creation where the actors' own 'writing' of the text is drawn from the improvisation and testing of the action on stage in front of an audience. Although the performance is divided into three parts, they are not traditional acts. Each part has a different story following the lives of the main characters through the twentieth century. The text is fragmented and the action in each part is independent from the others. Lepage has always said that for him theatre starts from action, and action is central to his creative process. However, the emphasis is on action that is fresh and immediate, not repeated and interpreted. The audience comes to see and follow the performer, who is discovering action in front of them (Lepage, 2005).

The six-hour version of *The Dragons' Trilogy* was originally performed by eight actors – all long-standing members of Théâtre Repère (including Lepage who also directed) – interpreting some 30 different characters. Subsequently the second version had eight actors who took on the developed characters and made them their own, adapting them to their own personalities and re-working the existing text. The story takes place over 80 years, framed by two appearances of Halley's Comet. The setting is a car parking lot, covered by sand, that is an 'archae-ological site' where the past is discovered, following the idea that memories – what happened in the past – were buried in the sand. The stage is rectangular in shape, covered with sand and outlined by a wooden walkway. The audience face one another on the traverse stage. They are visibly present as voyeurs/observers of the journey embarked on by the characters. Throughout the performance the parking lot trans-forms and becomes many different locations; however, the sand remains as a connecting device. The sandy parking lot, which covers the remains of Quebec's old Chinatown, is the departure point for a journey through different communities; a journey that will define the key events of the twentieth century's cultural integration in Canada. Through these events, we follow the lives of two Quebecker girls, Jeanne and Françoise; their children; Crawford the Englishman; Wong the Chinese and his son Lee; and three generations of Japanese women, all named Yukali. However, it is the events in Jeanne's and Françoise's lives, from childhood to adulthood and finally death, which connect all three parts of *The Dragons' Trilogy*.

The Prologue starts in the darkness with voices saying: 'I've never been to China' (*The Dragons' Trilogy*, 2005, 15) repeated in sequence in French, English and Chinese (Cantonese). As the dim shadowy lights slowly come up we see the contour of an old parking attendant who searches with a lamp through sand and audience. The voices off-stage continue: 'When I was young, there used to be houses here ...' (2005, 15) in English, French, and Chinese. Throughout this sound installa-tion, the parking attendant continues his search. He holds his lamp against an object he finds in the sand – it is a musical box in the shape of a glass ball. Meanwhile, the trilingual narration continues to describe the setting and introduce the play as if revealing a mystery: 'Look at the old parking lot attendant. He never sleeps. It seems as if he is the dragon. The dragon who watches over the gates to immortality. He is the dragon. And this is *The Dragons' Trilogy*' (2005, 18). The parking attendant enters a cabin, illuminated with intense light from the inside (Figure 3.1). Other characters slowly appear with their hands glued to the window of the cabin. The journey through time, which will take us through the life cycle of the individuals and communities, begins.

'THE GREEN DRAGON'

The first part of *The Dragons' Trilogy*, 'The Green Dragon' is set in Quebec City between 1932 and 1935. It takes the spectator to a very local setting of Quebec in the 1930s. The action takes place in enclosed interior locations — a laundry, a barber's store, a room and a basement. The characters constantly refer to a cold and wet environment. This is an entrenched community with high racial and religious prejudices. The space is fragmented through dim lights and shadows; it is deliberately

Figure 3.1 Scene from the end of the Prologue (first version) of *The Dragons' Trilogy*. Photo by Claudel Huot.

small, suffocating and narrow. The action starts with Jeanne and Françoise as young girls, playing in the sand (Figure 3.2). Using a pile of shoeboxes they recreate the shops in St Joseph Street, one of the main shopping streets in Quebec City. In their play they interact as grown-ups, resuming different characters. The shoebox is a store. One of the girls knocks on the box and the other lifts the lid as if opening a door, and they play a customer and merchant situation. Through this game, the audience is introduced to the social and cultural context of Quebec City in the 1930s.

Out of their game emerges a real character, Crawford, who walks on the set and is in St Joseph Street as if he is part of their play (Figure 3.3). He stops in front of a shoebox that represents a Chinese laundromat. This changes into a real situation as Crawford knocks at the door. He is an English shoe-salesman who was born in Hong Kong and has just arrived to Quebec City to set up his business. He is befriended by a Chinese laundryman, Wong, with whom he shares a passion for gambling. Crawford and Wong are also united by their position as the 'other', being culturally isolated in the society where they live. Crawford teaches Wong to play poker and, in exchange, Wong gives him a 'surprise' – he introduces Crawford to opium smoking (Figure 3.4). They set up poker gambling sessions with the locals, Lépin the undertaker and Morin the drunken barber (who is Jeanne's father). Jeanne has a boyfriend Bedard, disliked by

Figure 3.2 One of the earlier phases of *The Dragons' Trilogy* in 1986. Marie Brassard re-creates St Joseph Street by playing with sand and a toy car.

Figure 3.3 Crawford (Robert Lepage, in the first version of *The Dragons' Trilogy*) emerges as a real character out of a children's game (Marie Brassard and Marie Gignac) with shoeboxes. Photo by Claudel Huot.

Figure 3.4 Scene from the first version of *The Dragons' Trilogy*. Visions of China in Crawford and Wong's collective dream are seen in an opium den underneath the laundry. Photo by Claudel Huot.

her father, by whom she becomes pregnant. The 'Green Dragon' ends with Morin gambling away all his money, the barber shop and, finally, his pregnant daughter, who now has to marry Lee, Wong's son.

'THE RED DRAGON'

The second part, the 'Red Dragon', spans 1935 to 1955. It uses simultaneous fragmented events on stage, where different times and spaces overlap, showing parallel narratives. The 'Red Dragon' continues to follow events in the lives of Jeanne, Lee Wong, Françoise and Crawford, and is structured in two sections. The first covers 1935 to 1945. In the prologue we hear voices in French and English setting the scene in 1935 Toronto. This section starts with a scene without words that portrays Jeanne and Lee's domestic life. Jeanne is listening to a radio playing instrumental music from the song *Yukali tango*. The sound transforms the space, and we are now in a hotel room where the Japanese geisha Yukali is having sex with an American navy officer. She becomes pregnant and is ultimately rejected by the officer. This starts a new sub-narrative where we follow the life of Yukali, her daughter and granddaughter. The next scene is in a train where Françoise, who has joined the Canadian Army Women Corps, is on her way to Toronto to find Jeanne (who now lives there with her daughter Stella and her husband Lee). Françoise meets Crawford in the train. He now owns a shoe store in Toronto where Jeanne works. The section ends in 1945 at an army show in London, where Françoise sings a Christmas song to celebrate the end of the Second World War. Meanwhile Stella has been diagnosed with meningitis and Lee goes to Crawford to inform him that Jeanne will not be working at the shoe store any more since she has to look after Stella. The section ends in a skating ring. All the characters in the performance return simultaneously and perform their character's most expressive physical movements (Figure 3.5).

The second section takes place on 6 August 1955. Yukali announces in Japanese that it is ten years since the bombing of Hiroshima. We see Jeanne who, unable to look after her mentally disabled daughter, decides to send her to a hospital run by Catholic nuns in Quebec City. Yukali's narrative runs in parallel. Her daughter, now 20 years old, is writing to her American father and ceremonially burying his photo. The second section ends with Jeanne's suicide after discovering that she has incurable cancer.

'THE WHITE DRAGON'

Set in Vancouver in 1985 the third and final part, the 'White Dragon', reflects contemporary life, the mixing of cultures, travelling, comfort and anonymity. This section brings the life cycle of our main characters to a close. In the prologue, a voice announces the time every ten seconds in French, German, Japanese and English. This lasts for two minutes and amounts to twelve announcements. During each of

Figure 3.5 The skating ring made of sand and shoes, at the end of 'The Red Dragon' (first version), the second of the three Parts of *The Dragons' Trilogy*. Photo by Claudel Huot.

these announcements we see twelve physical images. We see all the characters doing short scores which last ten seconds each. The third part then starts in the departure lounge at Vancouver airport (Figure 3.6). Françoise is returning to Quebec City after visiting her son Pierre who has an art gallery in Vancouver. Pierre meets the third Yukali, also a painter, at the airport (see Figure 2.2). They start a relationship. Crawford, now totally dependent on opium, has made a film about his drug habits (Figure 3.7). During the passage of Halley's Comet, Crawford, who is in a wheelchair, sets himself on fire and dies (Figure 3.8). Stella is raped and killed in the hospital by another mental patient.

The stage space represents a non-location. It is not defined as in the previous parts. There are more abstract and neutral spaces – the airport, an art gallery, a cinema, a mountain, the hospital, an art gallery, an aeroplane. The enlargement of the space and the specific lighting that defines it become signs of universality and refinement. From the scene in the airport, the space grows to artistic exploration (through the installation show made of lights by one of the characters); it becomes the cosmos and then returns to the parking lot. The scenes in this part are fewer and longer, and the *mise-en-scène* takes up the

Figure 3.6 The airport in 'The White Dragon' (second version), the third of the three Parts of *The Dragons' Trilogy*. The wooden cabin is a duty-free shop. © photo: Érick Labbé.

Figure 3.7 Crawford (Tony Guilfoyle) in 'The White Dragon' (second version), the third of the three Parts of *The Dragons' Trilogy*. A film is projected live on the back screen. © photo: Érick Labbé.

Figure 3.8 Crawford's death in 'The White Dragon' (second version), the third of the three Parts of *The Dragons' Trilogy*, is symbolized by a burning wheelchair. © photo: Érick Labbé.

whole of the stage space. This part ends with an Epilogue which completes the cycle and brings us back to the Prologue. The play ends with the old parking lot attendant returning with the glass ball musical box in his hands, indicating the possibility of a new beginning. We hear the Chinese, Crawford's and Françoise's voices repeating the text from the beginning of the play, 'I've never been to China'. There is no end or resolution. The parking lot is a portal into the past where time is suspended. The past is buried in the sand, as a metaphor for the memories buried inside of us.

THE REHEARSAL PROCESS

The performance text of *The Dragons' Trilogy* is the outcome of a collectively devised process of stage-writing. Although the six original devisers are credited on the cover of the published play in 2005, this production has been always referred to as Lepage's *The Dragons' Trilogy*. In the tradition of director's theatre, Lepage, rather than the group of actor-authors who devised the material, became the recognizedlabel and identified author of this performance text. The fact is that the performance became internationally and critically renowned long before there was a published text. The production has been critically acknowledged not for the value of the dialogue or the literary qualities of the text, but for its imaginative and visually complex theatricality, multi-layered meanings and cinematic images, for which Lepage's directing was mainly credited.

As a published text, *The Dragons' Trilogy* is still more of a recording of the performance than a traditional text written by a playwright. Lepage's performance texts are not often staged by other directors or companies. (*The Seven Streams of the River Ota* had, in 2005, a very successful staging in Brazil, but the critics were divided over the production's authenticity, some claiming that it was just a remake of Lepage's staging). The understanding of Lepage's work as a director is inseparable from the group 'writing' process, and the devising of *The Dragons' Trilogy* combined the actor-author approach with a multi-disciplinary *mise-en-scène* where visual image and dialogue were intertwined into one expression. Lepage believes in the actor who is a storyteller, an author of their own text, someone who the audience will listen to. He says that, as a director, 'I try to help them tell the story and make it interesting; then they decide how to do it' (Lepage, 2002).

The development of *The Dragons' Trilogy* followed the working method of *The RSVP Repère Cycles*. The first performance cycle resulted in a ninety-minute production. The first open rehearsal took place in November 1985 at the small Implanthéâtre in Quebec City. This performance served as a resource for the second cycle, where the production developed from ninety minutes to three hours and had its open rehearsal in May 1986 (at the same venue). One month later it had further developed. The sections which were relevant to English characters and locations were developed and translated into English. This version premiered at the Du Maurier World Stage Festival in Toronto. As we have seen, when it opened in the final phase as a six-hour performance, in June 1987, it won Lepage the *Grand Prix* for directing. (This was the version that toured until 1991.) So we can see that the performance text transformed and developed over a period of three years. The growth from a ninety-minute to a six-hour production was due to the performance itself evolving out of actors' own writing and an ongoing devising process. Lepage was there to facilitate the creative process by framing and shaping the work as a stage image, selecting dramaturgical connections and new ideas and eliminating material that was not progressing the performance further.

We have seen how Lepage personalizes the creative process by making the relation between actor and resources central to his directing approach. As explained in chapter two, the resources could be physical (material objects) and emotional (stories, anecdotes or memories). To Lepage, a resource must be an impulse for action, 'a provocation rich in meaning that can inspire the group' to engage in an individual process (1999). More than anything else, resources must be concrete. If a deck of cards, for example, is used as a group resource, there will be different reactions and responses. As Lepage explains:

> With the group you play cards; you look at them; you explore them the way you want. People begin to talk about the cards. Someone will say they look like a family with the king being the father etc., someone else will see the opposition between black and red. Some will see death, others will see hazard. These are feelings, not ideas. One can't have an opinion about a deck of cards, and you can't discuss a sensation. I can't say to someone it is not true if he tells me that he sees the cards bleeding when he plays poker.
>
> (Lefebvre, 1987, 32)

Resources need a solid foundation – a parking lot covered in sand, or family stories or events remembered. They can also be well-known characters, or other arts or films. Whatever it is, the resource has to provide a group provocation so that each actor-author can create their own personal material. The collectively agreed starting resources for *The Dragons' Trilogy* were a parking lot in Quebec City where, according to Lepage's mythology, the old Chinatown used to be in the early twentieth century, and the idea that the performance would trace the Chinese community throughout the twentieth century – moving from Quebec City to Toronto and finishing in Vancouver (the three cities cited at the beginning of this chapter). Since *The Dragons' Trilogy* was originally supposed to be a collection of six solo-performances on the same theme, the starting resource served to unify individual performers' personal material and their research work. Therefore, these stimuli allowed each actor-author to establish their own interpretation and personal relation, and to see how these resources were relevant to their own experience. This process is not about factuality but fictionalizing what is real and personalizing it. Rémy Charest observes that the heart of Chinatown in downtown Quebec City was not in the area that was turned into a parking lot, but was what is now the area under an elevated highway (Charest, 2006). For Lepage, the parking lot (and for that matter the China itself) is a resource with which the actor-author can establish different personal reference points and use it according to their own needs:

> The China of the *Trilogy* was a China that suited what we wanted to say in the production. And the country itself is something like that, but it's also many other things. China has its smells, its textures, its rules, its sensations, none of which we know, but none of which we needed for the show. It's not important to be geographically precise. It's like our use of an anecdote: what's important is that it fits in the show.
>
> (Charest, 1997, 35–36)

Multi cultural performance and visual expressiveness, not cultural investigation in the ethnographic sense, are the main objectives of Lepage's creative process. Artistic and cultural traditions are changed once they are juxtaposed or interpreted by other cultures. This is relevant to both the form and content of *The Dragons' Trilogy*. The hegemonic supremacy of one culture is challenged by the newcomers (Morin loses his property and daughter to the Chinese laundryman; Bedard loses the woman he loves on a card game). What the Chinese are to the French, the French are to the English – foreigners with different traditions and languages. They are immigrants in different social circumstances in search of their identities. *The Dragons' Trilogy*, for better or worse, does not aim to explain what it means to be Chinese in Canada. Instead, China is a personal resource for the actor. Artistic license is consciously used to present a vision of being Chinese ('other' in a French-dominated Quebec), and how that progressed to a multi-cultural setting of contemporary Canada. Lepage's intercultural collage may be problematic and questionable, and was indeed challenged as 'cultural tourism' (Fricker, 2003), but even in its extreme manifestation it is only a theatrical reflection of a far more painfully real Americanization of the world and the legacy of a new western imperialism and neo-colonialism (spearheaded by the Bush-Blair coalition's 'war on terror').

In order to establish dramaturgical links and find new images and resources, during the devising process of *The Dragons' Trilogy* the group occasionally referred to Oriental traditions – that of *I Ching: The Book of Change* and the principle of **yin and yang**. *I Ching* helped in finding connections in the 'Valuaction' part of the creative cycle, the period when dramaturgical selection of the material is made, along with decisions of what to develop further and what to abandon. '*I Ching* provided us with the image of a well, which involves digging, seeking out the roots, the heart of things. So we understood that our characters had to dig inside themselves to find their own roots' (Charest, 1997, 99). The yin and yang helped provide a key element in the development of the characters – unity of oppositions. Lepage explains that in *The Dragons' Trilogy* everything they did had a 'feminine and masculine side ... we were playing with those ideas, making interesting characters so there is a male that has a feminine quality or a female that is extremely physically masculine' (1999).

As with Lepage's other original productions, numbers were an important dramaturgical device. The significance of the number three in this project came from the names of dragons in the Chinese card game of mah-jong. The game's cards or tiles were used as a metaphor for the three parts – Green, Red and White Dragon. Moreover, the rules of mah-jong reflect the overall dramaturgy of the play (discussed later in this chapter). Structurally the performance becomes a trilogy, not only consisting of three parts but also of three locations, three times and three sub-narratives. Lepage admits that, although most choices were made arbitrarily, 'when we began to do research about those cities [Quebec, Toronto and Vancouver], coincidences began to reveal themselves'(Lefebvre, 1987, 32). The Chinese community was more active in Quebec City at the beginning of the century, Toronto was important during the Second World War, and Vancouver is presently becoming one of the biggest Chinese settlements in North America. This coincided with the idea of placing the 'Green Dragon' section in Quebec, the 'Red Dragon' in Toronto and the 'White Dragon' in Vancouver. Group and individual research were important aspects in 'translating' what derived from intuition, spontaneous and accidental creativity. Lepage acknowledges that for coincidences to happen, he must listen to those he works with:

> I must let all kinds of exploration happen; I must liberate the longing of the people I work with have to play. I was working with six people and they had enough confidence in me to tell me their dreams, their ideas, to confide to me things that had no apparent relation to what we were doing but which would find their place later. But I know this dynamism is somewhat mysterious.
>
> (Lefebvre, 1987, 33)

Apart from establishing the starting spatial image for the devising process, it was important to discover emotional resources that could propel the action. Emotional resources do not have to come from grand narratives or big 'classical' stories. As Lepage often observes, they are all sorts of little stories about ordinary people that have a personal and, obviously, emotional connection with an individual performer. Emotional resources can be anecdotes, legends or personal experiences. It is a story that the performer can identify with and feel very excited by. The real-life story that became an emotional resource for the development of the main action in the first part of *The Dragons' Trilogy* originated from events close to Lepage's family. Marie Gignac, one of Lepage's principal collaborators and one of the creators of the project, explains:

> His mother when she was young lived in the Saint–Roch neighborhood of Quebec City, beside the Chinese quarter. One of her friends found she was pregnant at the age of sixteen, at the end of the 1920s. The father of this friend played a lot of cards with a Chinese man and owed him a large sum of money. This Chinese man wanted to get married … the man proposed to the father of this friend the following bet: 'If I win, I marry your daughter and wipe out all your debts; if I lose you owe me nothing.' He won and married this woman … The daughter of this woman, at the age of five, had meningitis and she had to be placed in a specialized institution at the age of twelve. She died there at forty, raped and murdered by another patient.
>
> (Gignac, 1987, 177–78)

This personal story was an emotional resource the group could collectively respond to. Likewise, using lyrics from the song *Yukali tango* became a resource for devising a whole narrative involving three generations of Japanese woman called Yukali. The story of these three women was the central narrative in 'The White Dragon'. Together with the space (the parking lot covered in sand) and the mah-jong game it was the reference point for the group's devising process.

One of the main objectives of Lepage's creative process is not to have pre-conceived ideas, or in fact any director's concept, before work with the actors starts. Rather, he wants to allow stories to come out through the actors' spontaneous playfulness and improvisations with the resources. Therefore, the performance text for *The Dragons' Trilogy* was an outcome of a work process where stories were discovered throughout the rehearsal process. As explained in chapter two, developing the narrative through phases was possible because performance can become the starting point in *The RSVP Cycles*. It is a resource from which a new creative cycle can be devised. Since the work is collectively devised, any improvisation or 'stage writing' done by an individual or a group of performers can become stimuli for another performer to create new material. This is how narratives are discovered through performance, by acting and observing the action, through individual and group creativity.

Lepage learned the process of personalizing material through writing one's own text in Alan Knapp's actor-creator workshops. As is usual in Lepage's practice, the material in *The Dragons' Trilogy* was improvised, and the scenes created by the actor-authors transcribed or video-recorded. It is interesting that the text remained essentially the same as it was discovered in the initial improvisations, and it does not change drastically in the final versions. In other of Lepage's devised projects such as *The Seven Streams of the River Ota* or *The Geometry of Miracles*, the text undergoes major changes and rewrites. The reason for this was that in *The Dragons' Trilogy* each actor-author originally established a personal reference point, finding material that was very close to their own experience yet related to the group's starting resources. The stories came from their own background and the life they were all very familiar with. When this is not the case, the group has to re-work and re-write the text. Over time, as the group goes further into the research material and finds out more about the lives of the characters that they are devising, the stories become more personalized.

Rebecca Blankenship, opera singer, actor and long-standing Lepage collaborator, observes that it is better for her as an actor if she remains an author during the performance:

> As soon as I start worrying about being an actor, then I go a step too far … I forget that I wrote it myself, and it's like trying to reinterpret yourself … We are all better off when we remember that we wrote it, and that we control it, and that it's part of our nature.
>
> (Blankenship, 1996)

Also, by being herself, she does not have to train her 'body memory' to adopt the circumstances of the character she plays but uses the natural reservoir of resources within her psychological make-up; it becomes natural for her because it is herself doing a scene. The actor's performance is not fixed or coded into a set pattern of actions. It is flexible and open, coming from the performer's own 'body memory'. Blankenship explains: 'Because they [emotions] come from such a natural place, so every night they come from that same place ... You do not have to get back to the source of how the writer or the composer has intended something to be. If you've written it yourself you're always there' (Blankenship, 1996).

PLAYING WITH MATERIAL OBJECTS

It is important to understand the context of playing that is so fundamental to Lepage's theatre practice. Lepage, in common with other twentieth-century practitioners – Jacques Copeau, Jacques Lecoq, Ariane Mnouchkine, Peter Brook, **Clive Barker**, Pina Bausch and Anna Halprin – places imagination, improvisations and physical expressiveness at the heart of the creative process. The concept of the director/actor as an interpreter of the playwright's text was increasingly abandoned from the 1960s onwards, in favour of collective performance exploring group response and pre-rehearsal techniques as a new vocabulary for performance. Creating the dramatic text during workshops/rehearsals through the actors' improvisations became a way of making theatre. The actors were empowered to be creators and not just mere interpreters of the text. Performance text liberated the actor from servitude to the written text and from an imposed *mise-en-scène* that arrived from pre-conceived concepts.

In discussions, Lepage often reinforces the idea of 'acting as playing'. He points out that we have lost the notion of acting as a spontaneous process, and that player has become actor, a serious and established professional (Lepage, 2002). Lepage rejects the professionalism of traditional theatre, where the joy of discovery through process is burdened with psychological and intellectual clichés, over-analytical and conceptual approaches and an orientation towards achieving a pre-determined final product. Instead, Lepage's performance practice relies on provoked chaos, chance, actors' personal material and playfulness. The way the spirit of playing is captured through creative process is embedded in a 'final' performance. For Lepage, playing becomes a way of theatre-making rather than serious professionalism and working towards the perfection of the final product. Both theatrically and as a creative process Lepage makes actors playing with material objects central to his performance practice. Lepage sees his job as providing an interesting playground for the actors.

> As a child I always played with the box the toy came in much more than the actual toy. Creating a piece should include the childish spirit – when people have fun you feel the warmth of the emotions and the interactions. Then you bring it to the audience and it has to be a playground for them.
>
> (Hemming, 1991)

The idea that theatre is a playground is very relevant to both the way the rehearsal process takes place and the way the performance asks the audience to engage with it. Similarly to Keith Johnstone's ideas on improvisation embedded in his Theatresports, Lepage's notion of spontaneous live action that happens at the moment refers to the audience's and performers' simultaneous involvement in the discovery of what is happening on stage (Johnstone, 1987). Anything can happen at any point. It is a process where the past (where we have been) is clear, but not the future (where are we going). As a director, Lepage ensures that the actors are in an environment where they are sur- rounded with material they can play with, objects with which they can interact and, most importantly, start performing with. The choice of resources – objects – which are used depends on the performer's ability to establish a relation with them. The resource has to be a point of reference for the actor, so that they can establish the inner relation with it. If not, the actor looks for another resource to engage with, changing and adapting it, as in any game where choices are made at the moment. The parking lot that covers the remains of the commu- nity is a spatial resource that could be used as a collective reference, where each member of the group can find something hidden in the sand, giving each of them something to work/play with.

In developmental psychology, playing is considered the preferred orientation for children to discover reality as it is a voluntary, sponta- neous and pleasant activity (Piaget, 2000). Piaget's symbolic play hap- pens when young children are able to differentiate the 'signifier' from what is signified (Piaget, 2000, 58). It shows that children can sub- stitute one object for another through imitation, and that the meaning prevails over the physical attributes, in a way that anything can stand for something else. Lepage's playing with objects and their transformation is an extension of symbolic play, where the actor, like a child, plays with objects and gives them characteristics that come out of a game. Stimulating actors to create through games that used objects symbolically was essential to the way *The Dragons' Trilogy* was devised. The symbolic use of objects depends on how the object is used by actors. On stage, objects are not defined by their 'reality' or material qualities, but through the performer's appropriation of them. Therefore, the actor's interpretation of the object is different from its implied meaning. One object can have many different meanings depending on the context in which it appears. And, in turn, the way the actors relate to the objects determines the way the audience perceives them.

The *mise-en-scène* for *The Dragons' Trilogy* was created through actors playing with objects. In the first scene of 'The Green Dragon', two actor creators (Marie Brassard and Marie Gignac in the original 1987 version) are playing as two young girls with shoeboxes creating a street. In the previous rehearsal phases the actors were playing with sand and a toy car, out of which a real car came carrying Crawford (see Figure 3.3). The object that is used as a toy is then transformed through their game to 'represent' the houses and the actual St Joseph Street in Quebec City. The children's play becomes the supplement for the actual/objective presentation of the scene. Throughout their game they are setting a story from which the actual characters appear. In fact, we can say that in *The Dragons' Trilogy* the scenes are devised around a number of key objects – sand, a cabin, a lamp post, a glass musical ball, shoeboxes, shoes, a suitcase, a barber's chair, laundry, a razor blade, a barrel, an umbrella, a kitchen table, chairs, opium, ropes, a white canvas, origami, a dactylographer, a bicycle, a toy car, a wheelchair, a car, candles and an aeroplane propeller.

The objects are used as metaphors to represent the plurality of meanings required by the theatrical 'language'. The objects on stage are transformed into a polyvalent theatrical sign through the actors' interactions. The objects initially used by Jeanne and Françoise in their game, the shoeboxes, stay on the stage throughout the first section to signify a row of shops and houses on the main street. Likewise, the cabin remains physically a cabin throughout the performance, but its meaning transforms. The actors are using it as a guard's booth on the parking lot, a time machine, a laundry, a cellar, a roof from where to observe the stars, the place where Françoise takes a dactylographic lesson, an airport shop, the door of the house. The objects do not appear throughout the performance in any particular order, but in different contexts defined by the performers' actions. For example, a white cloth is used several times in *The Dragons' Trilogy*. At the beginning, it is linked to the tradition of the Chinese laundryman. Next, we find it as a screen that allows the projection of the characters' dreams. Further on, it is associated with sails and voyages, as part of a junk (boat). As the performance develops, it is used to show the bloodstains that confirm Stella's death.

In the scene where Morin the barber is shaving the young Bedard for the first time, the ritual is completed with the use of real life objects – a razor, foam, hot towel, lotions, etc. The whole process is ceremonially 'presented', relying on these materials as 'representative' of the action. The scene that concludes 'The Green Dragon', the poker game, happens on a turned barrel with the players miming the game and the cards in a stylized way, banging with their palms on the metal barrel as if drumming, increasing the rhythm as the game progress. However, they use real-life objects as the stake – Jeanne is real and the barber's chair 'represents' the shop. Betting is the event, so the emphasis is on what is at stake, what will be lost or gained. Drunken Morin looses everything in the poker game to Wong. The finale of the scene is visual image/metaphor, where Jeanne sits in a barber's chair, mounted on the top of the barrel, swinging in a circular motion when moved by Wong and his son Lee.

It is not only physical objects that have this quality to transform, connect or become symbols and images as spatial metaphors. Lepage also uses the performers' bodies and their physical presence as symbols and images. For example, Jeanne in 'The Red Dragon' is associated with her childhood love from 'The Green Dragon' – Bedard – either as Jeanne's vision or as part of a dream sequence (riding a bicycle or physically interacting with her but invisible to others on the stage). Section one in 'The Red Dragon' culminates with all the characters on the stage simultaneously, but in their own time, re-living key events/moments from the past. They are images locked in a dance routine repeating single actions in a dream-like state. This group of individual scores transforms the shoe store into a skating ring, where skaters destroy shoes by skating over them collectively – creating an image of the devastation that the Second World War inflicted upon civilians and humanity.

The scene in 'The White Dragon' in which Crawford's aeroplane crashes provides another good example of the transformation of material objects and use of physical expressiveness. The pilot comes on stage with a big black suitcase that he puts on the sand. He lies flat on his stomach on the suitcase extending his arms and legs, a turning fan above him creates the living engine of the plane, and the Christmas lights in the sand (used in the previous scene to represent an art installation in Pierre's studio) become an aerial view of Vancouver from the airplane. The bodies of the other actors are used to create the silhouettes of skyscrapers. The event of the crash constructed in theatrical space, through the integration of material objects and the performers' bodies, illustrates a fundamental principle of Lepage's thinking – namely that communication with audience is through a combination of visual (physical/media) images and verbal language.

Another example is the scene in 'The Red Dragon' where Lee discovers that Stella has meningitis. During rehearsals the actors improvised on how to communicate this information to the audience. The verbal text was very melodramatic, and when played for its psychological values, as Tony Guilfoyle (the English actor playing Crawford in the 2003 version) observes, 'It sounded as a bad soap opera' (Guilfoyle, 2006). After various improvisations with the text and the information that needed to be conveyed using verbal language, Lepage found the solution through the symbolic use of objects, the space and the actor's body to communicate this event. On one end of the stage there was just a table representing a domestic setting – the kitchen where Lee and Jeanne were. On the other end of the stage there were four chairs representing Crawford's shoe shop. Lee's character wants his wife to stay at home and look after their ill daughter. Lepage instructed the actor playing Lee to cross the stage to inform Crawford that his wife can no longer work for him and that she will be staying at home. Lee then takes each of the four chairs from the shoe store and puts them around the kitchen table. The last chair to be taken is the one where Crawford was sitting. Lee pushes this chair under Jeanne for her to sit on, effectively locking her with the table. With this physical action she was metaphorically imprisoned in the house, losing connection with the outside world. Her life has been changed forever. 'Improvisations are not always about linear dialogue, they can be about visual things, juxtapositioning things where lots of action is going on at once, and Robert is good in creating meaning thorough layering' (Guilfoyle, 2006).

Lepage's performance texts have often been criticized for their lack of literary values, their naïvety or for clichés, often having a dialogue close to 'TV soaps'. The non-textual position of his theatre is evident and it is something that Lepage has never attempted to hide. Being an actor himself, coming from a background of collective creation and being very good at improvised short stand-up routine (often using improvised comedy), Lepage believes in the actor-creator who can write their own text regardless of whether they are a good or bad writer. A text that comes from their own experiences gives the actors direct connection with the material. The effectiveness of Lepage's performance does not depend on literary values of a text but on the interplay between various theatrical elements – resources (space, objects, images, sounds, etc.) where dialogue is only one of the points of communication and artistic expression.

OBSTACLES

While studying with Alan Knapp, Lepage was introduced to the method of creating by imposing self-limitations and obstacles. We have seen that Lepage's practice is about process and not product, and that this process is shaped through spontaneous and free playfulness. However, by establishing a set of limitations and obstacles, self-imposed by each actor-creator, Lepage creates a dynamism within the work process. This dynamism is shaped by two opposing forces – restrictions and freedom. Lepage explains that, for Knapp, the creator has to be 'in a state analogous to a lemon being squeezed. The creator must define limits, bounds, constraints and obey them until creation oozes out' (Lefebvre, 1987, 33). One of the principles that Lepage retained from Knapp is that the more obstacles you impose on yourself, such as limitations in time and space, the more the work and the performance will benefit. The purpose of these obstacles is to act as an inner stimulant for the actor-creator.

Lepage believes that every actor should have a physical challenge. Like acrobats, actors have to set up the individual obstacles that they have to meet. 'When you're aware of the challenge, the Olympian nature of theatre, the human beings on stage acquire a kind of nobility, a divinity. Our goal is Mount Olympus – not a gymnasium in Athens, but the place where the gods meet' (Charest, 1997, 85). Lepage claims that it is important for him to trust his own instincts and give himself entire freedom to create. This process is a dialectical opposition, with obstacles and imposed limitations on one side, and free creative energy and improvised action on the other. Out of the interaction between these two forces, the dynamism of the *mise-en-scène* is conceived.

The first phase of rehearsals for *The Dragons' Trilogy* lasted three weeks, and the main purpose was to research and write, try the scores and explore newly found resources. Lepage started the initial rehearsals by asking each actor-creator to bring their own personal material, their feelings, dreams and ideas regarding the established resource. This in itself is an obstacle – each actor is a researcher and improviser, finding, shaping and presenting their own material to the group. This individual material is then collectively used, and the group (or often Lepage) selects what is valuable to keep and develop further. Lepage explains that

> the direction and blocking, the *mise-en-scène*, is as eloquent as the text, sometimes more so. The actors' performance expresses at times the *mise-en-scène* rather than the text … If the *mise-en-scène* of *The Dragons' Trilogy* – the show's principal defining element – doesn't hold up, we have no reason to tell the story a second time. If we were to remount it, I would restructure some elements and stage them differently, rather than simply do a revival.
>
> (Charest, 1997, 162)

Through this exploratory phase, the structure of the narrative slowly emerged, but it was not crucial to find it before the first open rehearsal in 1985. The open rehearsals serve for the group to perform the material they have been working on in front of an audience and see how fragmented scores fit together. In this way, this set meeting with the audience is an imposed restriction and the group works towards it.

Every improvisation of scores in *The Dragons' Trilogy* is organized around a set of obstacles that results in a new action. In *Robert Lepage – Connecting Flights,* Lepage gives a good example of how limitations stimulate the creative process. In the scene from 'The Red Dragon' when Jeanne and Sister Marie are about to put Stella in a mental institution, the same actress plays Stella and Sister Marie. Since there is no time for a costume change, the transformation has to be done in front of an audience as part of the stage action. Jeanne removes the Sister's clothes, one garment at a time, and puts them in her daughter's suitcase. In this process she transforms her into Stella. To justify this transformation, a new story was invented with a whole new set of symbols, using objects/props to expand the vocabulary of theatrical expressiveness. The group created a whole ritual around this movement, and came up with a new ritual where the nun's cap became the symbol for the mind, the surplice a symbol for the heart and so on. This approach was then used in other scenes where live transformation was done in front of the audience. All this was created to overcome the obstacle of having no time for the actor to change costumes. A new scene that transformed one event into another was introduced. Lepage integrates the scene changes and transitions into the performance action, making an aesthetic expression out of simple transactions such as costume changes.

For the second version in 2003, Lepage worked with a new group of actors – Sylvie Cantin, Jean-Antoine Charest, Simon Chartand, Hughes Frenette, Tony Guilfoyle, Eric Leblanc, Veronika Makdissi-Warren and Emily Shelton. Marie Gignac, who was a deviser from the original version, was to provide dramaturgic assistance. Under the technical production of *Ex Machina*, the group reworked the 1987 performance. Actors were given a transcript of the original performance and shown a six-hour video. The existing characters were reference points but also obstacles – the new actors had to create their own characters rather than imitate the ones from the recording of the first version.

Lepage is often involved in acting in his devised performances at the early phases of writing; like other actors in the collective process he creates his own character(s), before the performance is more developed and needs his full attention as an outside eye. In the first version Lepage devised and acted the character of Crawford, later played by Tony Guilfoyle in the 2003 version. Guilfoyle is a classically trained actor with substantial experience in devising, who had collaborated with Lepage on three productions. It is interesting to observe the differences in the creation of the two versions of Crawford, in order to understand how Lepage uses obstacles in his creative process. Having limited time to rehearse before opening the show at the Festival de Théâtres des Ameriques in 2003 in Montreal (and going on a subsequent international tour), Guilfoyle had to work within a specific frame dictated by time constraints and by the fact that the existing material (the transcribed text) determined the contours and content of the future performance.

The new cycle of *The Dragons' Trilogy* was not a remounting of the same old show with a new cast, nor was it a staging of a dramatic text with a new directorial concept. This was an *RSVP* take on a performance that was to be re-developed. The 2003 version used actors that brought their different experiences into the interpretation of the performance text, thus making the performance their own. Knapp's notion of actor/creator was implemented in the sense that the actors created their own performance using the previous performance as a resource. Lepage's Crawford was an Englishman who is an outsider, a displaced person born in Hong Kong, coming to start his business in Quebec City and subsequently settling down in Toronto. Lepage identifies with the position of outsider. Growing up in a bi-lingual family, he was aware of the displacement an Anglophone person feels in a predominantly francophone environment such as that of Quebec in the 1930s. Crawford's friendship with Wong, who is also 'other' to the francophone centre, is a logical consequence of Crawford's position. Lepage's Crawford was nostalgic and lovable, a comic version of the cliché of a colonial Englishman.

Lepage had three years to develop Crawford as a character. Guilfoyle had to respond to the obstacle of having an existing score and developed performance text with an already finished character. Rather than working from the existing character, Guilfoyle used this as a starting resource to develop his own Crawford, consequently changing the performance. Since Lepage wanted to tour the 2003 re-staging of *The Dragons' Trilogy* as a finished product, he did not allow Guilfoyle to use his own scenes and text for Crawford's character. Rather, he wanted Guilfoyle to keep the existing material but to adjust it to himself without entirely changing it. Unlike Lepage's Crawford, presented from an outside perspective of colonial Englishness, Guilfoyle's Crawford (being connected to his own experiences) had more depth and personal story. Guilfoyle was aware that the performance would play in London, bringing his Crawford in front of a home audience well aware of all the intricacies of English colonialism in its past and present forms. Guilfoyle's Crawford comes to Quebec City with the attitude of someone who has arrived to change the world, bringing with him all the arrogance and pretentiousness of colonial presence and class structures. However, he is attempting to 'colonize' French-speaking Quebec, and ends up becoming close to the Chinese immigrant community as he is also an 'other' to the mainstream, mainly small-minded Quebeckers.

Crawford becomes a drug addict and a documentary filmmaker, and finally sets himself on fire by throwing petrol on himself as a plane which is going to Hong Kong crashes. For Guilfoyle, Crawford's death and the aeroplane crash symbolize the end of the Empire (then British, now American). In the first version Crawford dies while flying to his place of birth, Hong Kong. However, in the second version, Guilfoyle decided that Crawford dies because he is ready to die, his time has come, and therefore he commits suicide by setting his wheelchair on fire. The new ending of Crawford's character is montaged into a single scene with the airplane crash, juxtaposing both actions simultaneously into one meaning.

The audience's interpretation is not based on the events and their connection in a linear cause-effect plot, but on the editing of actions, as in film, and the juxtaposition of text, sound, physical movement and images in space within the whole of the performance. The fact that the building blocks for the *mise-en-scène* are not founded on one overall narrative but actor-authors' scores that are independent and flexible units, each having its own story, allows autonomy in the associations and structuring of a performance. These associations have a freedom similar to that of children's games. One material object can serve many ideas/meanings that can reflect on each other, thus creating a number of other meanings like the reflections in a hall of mirrors.

GAMES SESSIONS

From the very start of *The Dragons' Trilogy* – the search with the lamp through the sand and the audience, the overlapping sounds and voices in different languages, the cabin magically lit from inside with different characters appearing around it – a game of discovery was initiated where fantasy and mystery were essential parts. The story takes us through different times and spaces in a simultaneous presentation of what is real and imagined, creating a collage of memories, dreams, hallucinations and rituals. As with the mah-jong game, a sense of mystery and unpredictability is at the centre of the theatre game that performers engage with. This can be extended to the way Lepage sees theatre as a whole, as a puzzle that is being solved throughout the process whose mystery is resolved only at the end. For Lepage, this is the basic connection between actor and audience – the spectators are observing people empowered by the process of discovery that is taking place at that very moment.

Playing games comes from the human ability to do different activities by using imagination and mimetic skills. This is the basis for learning and understanding processes. This ability to play is generally used in devising theatre as the starting point to create a performance. Theatre games were important for the creation of the performance text of *The Dragons' Trilogy*, and for Lepage as a director. What is interesting about Lepage is that he develops performance by playing in front of an audience where actors are involving audience in their game. 'I am trying to find a way of devising work that gives the impression that people are playing, and you are inventing a game much more than a script, and you end up writing things on the day after the closing of the show' (McAlpine, 1996, 135).

Clive Barker's theory of theatre games, which explores the actor's creative process through games, can be applied to Lepage's method of devising and playing to understand the creative process of *The Dragons' Trilogy*. Lepage shares Barker's view of theatre as a game session. They share the view that the outcome, both in performance and in games, has to be unpredictable. The audience has to be involved in the suspense and thrill of the game. They should be made another partner or a player. The key question that Barker wants to answer is how self-conscious actions (playing for someone who is observing) are turned into a 'non-reflective body/think mechanism' (spontaneous playing as children do in their games). Lepage believes that playing frees actors from restrains of 'professionalism', of a product-based theatre, and allows them to be spontaneous and playful. Barker sees theatre games as a means of releasing emotional energy and social inhibition. This helps the actor to substitute 'the pain of learning' with 'the joy of re-discovery' (Barker, 1989, 64). He explains that, 'Children's games are a readily accessible, and seemingly acceptable, framework for releasing physical and emotional energy. Pressure is released, and the human being is to some extent made free, in a framework which is not susceptible to social criticism' (Barker, 1989, 64).

Barker names five purposes of the game sessions used to create a spontaneous genuine response in actors and the audience (Barker, 1989, 65–66). We will apply these purposes to elements used for *The Dragons' Trilogy* such as the mah-jong game and *I Ching*, but also the searching in a sand-covered parking lot, to reveal something of the actor's performance and to open up new possibilities. The game session has to:

1   Lead the actors to physical experiences and sensations that would otherwise not be directly accessible to them. Beginning to devise

from one starting resource, bringing their personal response to it and collectively sharing their individual improvisations and scores is a useful way of materializing internal feelings and finding new possibilities for expression.

2 Initiate a process of self-awareness and discovery in the actor. By playing games and also using objects, the actor engages beyond conscious thinking of what needs to be done, and opens up creative potentials from the subconscious.

3 Explore a shared body of experience, which could build relationships within the group, thus developing the performance which is made by an actor-author from their own experiences. This is based on a collective playing, where the game provides a common denominator for the group, in which a collective exploration is turned into a communicable experience.

4 Create a vocabulary that can unify various scores in performance. This means that the game session has to be both a theatrical style and a frame for the work, which can be applied to the individual and collective scores.

While devising, Lepage uses games to release the actors' inhibitions. He creates an environment that resembles a playground with various gadgets and objects that provide stimuli to help the actors. In this playground, actors can engage in improvisations without any conscious objectives or censorship and can release their inner child. This approach allows performers to be spontaneous and harness creative chaos to liberate the group's unconscious creativity, from which the material for the performance is drawn. By participating 'unselfconsciously' in game sessions, the actors reveal their own personality. This idea relates to Lepage's notion of liberating the performers to respond to their own need for creation. The audience is 'invited' to witness this playfulness, often discovering the outcomes at the same time as the actors.

PLAYING MAH-JONG

Chance and collective interplay are important features of the mah-jong game that was used as the creative principle in *The Dragons' Trilogy*. Each of the three Parts is, in theme and narrative, related to the symbols from mah-jong. Natalie Rewa explains how Lepage developed the stage imagery and the narrative of Jeanne and Françoise's lives by applying symbolism from mah-jong:

> The green dragon, ideogrammatically water and spring, is theatrically presented as the naïvety of childhood; the fire and summer of the red dragon are presented in terms of the conflicts of adult lives, including those of war; and the air and autumn of the white dragon are portrayed as the calm of the middle age and the spirituality of art.
>
> (Rewa, 1990, 150–51)

Like mah-jong, the dramaturgy of *The Dragons' Trilogy* depends on the connections between the different cards/parts, which make full sense once all three dragons are placed together. Each player in the game represents one side of the world, and their seating arrangements are made according to the different cardinal points (east, south, west and north). East starts the game, and it is believed that this is the best position, while the west would be the worst. The cycle of mah-jong is completed after four rounds when all four sides of the world have had their turn to start the game first. The three dragons – green, red, and white – are considered to be the best cards because they give more points, and when they are collected the player does not have to be concerned about which side of the world he is sitting on.

The principles of mah-jong were also important for the space. The transformation of the sandy parking lot and the discovery of what is hidden throughout the development of the performance had the logic of the card game. At the beginning of the play, the parking lot hides all the mysteries that will be revealed to the audience and performers. Likewise, the game has closed cards, which are unknown to the players/performers and must be figured out as the game/performance develops. The game is seen as a magical event in which personal superstitions plays an important role. Players have to determine their position in regard to other players, and the development of the game depends on how well the players can read one another's strategy.

Indeed, Lepage's rehearsal process is like a game that provides an environment and rules, within which the actors/creators can play and discover their space, characters and where the justification for the devised narrative can be found. Both the card game and the rehearsal process are unpredictable, and although there are set rules the result can vary.

The performance of *The Dragons' Trilogy* was also a combination of various rituals. Lepage's re-enactment of different ceremonies as a set of rules has the tangibility of ritual theatre. He indicates that 'the ritual theatre makes you live it [performance], makes you take part in it' (Carson, 1993, 329). In *The Dragons' Trilogy* 'daily rituals' are appropriated as a form of regulated conventions – from shaving, a poker game, a theatre of moving shadows, to the explanation of aircraft regulations, an art installation, the mah-jong and yin and yang. All of these 'rituals' become part of the performance.

Using the principles of mah-jong and appropriating them into a performance reflects a common approach in Lepage's theatre. He often takes other arts and cultures as theatre resources – objects to play with – and makes them into material for game-performance. The object, in this case the card game, changes its original cultural context into a new set of implied meanings needed for the performance. Lepage openly uses cultural clichés, particularly of Eastern and Oriental traditions and characters, as resources. He uses other cultures from his position and own cultural context. The term 'Oriental' for Lepage, as for the West, represents something that is romantic, exotic, mysterious and definitely different from the western approach to life.

THE AUDIENCE RESPONSE AS A RESOURCE

In Canada, the theatricality of Lepage's *The Dragons' Trilogy* was generally perceived (and praised by critics) as the development of a new theatre language, as a new Quebec theatre that could transcend linguistic and cultural boundaries. The search for a new more international way of communicating with the world through theatre performance was an important political concern for French-speaking Quebec in the late 1980s. On the other side of the Atlantic, when *The Dragons' Trilogy* was performed in London's Riverside Studios, the production was generally received very favourably by audiences and critics mainly because of its internationalism and intercultural references. The plural cultural co-existence in the performance where characters speak English, French, Chinese and Japanese is a metaphor for the world at large, and was a favoured topic of the intercultural discourse among critics and scholars at the end of the 1980s. The intercultural discourse was particularly fashionable with London audiences, who accepted Lepage and gave him a cult following. However,

Lepage is at home with audiences in many parts of the world. The explanation for this could be found in the openness of his performances to various cultural interpretations.

As his performances tour, each audience contributes to the understanding of the performance with something they 'read' into the narrative. In *The RSVP Cycles* the audience, as participants, is asked to respond to the performance/rehearsal. In *The Dragons' Trilogy,* this transcultural communication was made possible by the flexibility of the resources, which allowed for a variety of interpretations of the narration depending on the audience's experience. When the production was performed in Toronto, the reference to Chinese was understood as a symbolic representation of the position of the Quebeckers in Canada. On the other hand, outside of Canada, the reference to the Chinese became representative of the Asian cultural minority in Canada. As the narrative progresses through the development of the performance, the integration of cultures in *The Dragons' Trilogy* creates an intercultural milieu. Therefore, towards the end of the performance, the mixture of other cultural references creates a more integrated society.

Marie Gignac indicates that the group made minor modifications to the text when it was played in front of an English-speaking audience. However, since the show was in a plurality of languages, this did not affect the performance. Each audience could find something in the performance. Gignac explains that

> the play is received in a different way depending on the country. In Ireland, for example, people reacted a lot to maternity, to pregnancy, and little Stella had a big impact on the audience. In New York people were astonished by how simple the performance is.
>
> (Carson, 1993, 329)

Like geography, communities are important for setting the scores in *The Dragons' Trilogy.* The performance moves through Chinese communities in Canada, from the beginning of the twentieth century in Quebec City, to Toronto in the 1940s and 1950s, and finally to Vancouver's multi-cultural milieu at the end of the millennium. The sand pit was used as a location where communities are constructed through actors' personal resources – anecdotes and memories that connect them with a particular time and community. Out of these very personal and local reflections, different themes (concerning the discovery of global, cultural and personal identity) emerged, which had universal relevance for a global audience. The fact that these themes found world-wide appeal, regardless of their cultural or linguistic diversity, points to the international and human approach of Lepage's theatre and its engagement with the fundamental questions of our existence – how do the past and our memories shape our present moment, who are we and where are we going?

From the beginning to the end of *The Dragons' Trilogy* an important line, 'Je ne suis jamais allée en Chine' (*I have never been to China*) echoes the motive that hovers above the performance – the displaced in the search for identity. The reflections on the mode of existence, which are never complete, are presented through a hallucinatory vision, a dream of mythical China, which is different from any knowledge of the real China. The characters never reach China, or Hong Kong. They remain outside, telling the story form the point of view of the displaced. The myth of the Orient, the term 'China', becomes the supplement for the 'dream world', a fantasy that has never been achieved but always pursued. The distinct cultural perspectives (French, English, Chinese and Japanese) derive from this search for their own belongings. The cultural clashes are the outcome of that search, of the attempt to find what is missing in their lives, the attempt to live the dream. It is the vision of 'others' (cultures) in which all participants are estranged from their own individual and cultural identities, becoming a group portrait of their differences. They are all immigrants in their own social and cultural environment.

The response of the audience and critics worldwide was focused on the simplicity and imaginative theatricality of *The Dragons' Trilogy* and its ability to communicate with audiences internationally, and to transmit a story regardless of the linguistic barriers. The group's references to history, traditions, cultures and languages found resonance in the audience. In this performance, Lepage's transformative, multi-disciplinary and multi-cultural *mise-en-scène* employs a plurality of channels to communicate with international audiences, inviting technology, media and other arts into the theatrical space.

CONCLUSION

The Dragons' Trilogy had amazingly vibrant and critically successful production cycles spanning over two decades. It promoted Lepage as a new international director with an interesting, new and powerfully visual theatricality. The developmental phases of *The Dragons' Trilogy* were characterized by exploration and transformation, culminating in the final phase which took the world of theatre by surprise in 1987. However, at the time, critics and audiences alike did not understand Lepage's 'work in progress' process. They responded to the final outcome as presented in the festivals as a finished artwork. From the rehearsal process to the development of the performance, from the audience's reflection to the different cultural receptions, the common denominator is the transformability of the theatre action and narrative. It is not surprising then to find out that Lepage received very mixed and generally negative criticism for the first phases of his next major epic project, *The Seven Streams of The River Ota* (1994–1996). His solo show *Elsinore* (1995) was cancelled in 1996 when it was due to open the International Festival in Edinburgh. The performance text is not always ready for the audience, especially when the audience expects to see a finalized performance that is actually just a number of different improvised scores (scenes).

By exploring *The Dragons' Trilogy* performance we can observe that, depending on the actors' intentions on-stage, resources can have multiple meanings. In Lepage's devising process all the theatrical elements that make the performance environment (physical action, space, objects, visual projections, sound, verbal text, etc.) are equally important for the creation of the performance text. This means that the purpose of directing is not to translate the written text (since there is none), but to facilitate performance text based on theatricality, where the language of the stage is the main artistic expression. Performers' appropriation of the resources on the stage is the main alphabet of that language, where the performance is 'written' through the process of constant transformations of the space, action and images until the right expression and communication with the audience is discovered. These visual images are often implemented through the most simple collage of technical means (overhead, slide, 16mm and video projections and computer cameras for live feed) and actors' improvisations, but with the most thrilling aesthetic results.

In respect to the actors' personalization of the material in the original version of *The Dragons' Trilogy,* Lepage explains that some scores were continuously changed while for others the group would improvise once and record the material that would remain unchanged most of the time. The group would correct a few details in later rehearsals, but the captured essence of the scenes would fit within what the group wanted to do. Lepage believes that this is because the material had a personal resonance for everyone in the group, because the performance revolved around their lives and the lives of their parents and grandparents in the city they all knew very well (Charest, 1997, 100). It is a subjective material made of local stories that was internationally accessible through improvisations that included the audience responses, with a theatrical vocabulary that substituted verbal language with the language of the stage founded on visual images and actor-authors writing their own stories.

PRACTICAL WORKSHOPS AND REHEARSAL TECHNIQUES

INTRODUCTION

This chapter demonstrates workshop and rehearsal techniques relevant to Lepage's performance practice, and is divided into seven sessions:

1 Workshop conditions – preparing the scene
2 The body – physical action
3 The space – the performer's environment
4 The objects – playing and games
5 The scores – solo and group scenes
6 Montage – editing narratives
7 Text – working from fixed text.

It is important to note that what I describe here are not exercises in the traditional sense of actor-training, but rather sessions of a workshop process that will give an insight into Lepage's creative process. The aim of the workshops is to produce individual or group material for a devised performance, starting from a free-style improvisation as used in Lepage's performance practice. Lepage's rehearsal techniques position the actor as a writer of their own text through improvisation. Lepage's actors may not produce great literature, but they have to be skilful in improvisation. The workshop sessions can be used to learn improvisation as well as being a way through which you can devise a performance. The exercises start from personal and inner focus with the emphasis on body and physical expression and progress to group and outer focus, interacting, improvising and working from text.

Because Lepage is a theatre-maker, not a pedagogue, and is not concerned with training his actors, there is no published record of his rehearsal techniques (apart from literal descriptions of individual rehearsals) or a systematized actors training method. There are hours of video recordings of rehearsals where actors are devising performance, but there is no visible pre-rehearsal actor's training behind the creation of the performances. The background of the workshops described here and exercise techniques that follow are founded on Anna Halprin's *RSVP Cycles*, Alain Knapp's workshops for actors as authors of their own text, Keith Johnstone's experience with Theatresports (which is very similar to the Ligue National d'Improvisation) and exercises coming from Jacques Lecoq's training (which Lepage studied at the Conservatoire d'art dramatique de Québec). The re-creation and adaptation of these workshops and exercises is partly based on my own experience of teaching Lepage's devising process, for more than ten years, in undergraduate and postgraduate practical courses in the UK, Canada and Brazil.

1 WORKSHOP CONDITIONS

It is helpful if the group of participants in these workshops have their own project in mind and have a personal interest in making it. For Lepage's performance practice it is essential that performers are authors, who have a personal connection with the material they bring into rehearsal. It is important to have open feedback sessions after every workshop, as the group's response to what happened during the workshop is as valid as the material presented on stage.

There is no final destination or pre-conception about where the project has to go and what will be the final outcome. The performance is open to change throughout the workshop/rehearsal. It is about discovering through process, not building blocks. The improvisers are not looking towards the future but are aware of everything that is going on around them at the moment of improvisation. The material is generated from within the performer, but it is shaped and transformed through the collective process. The performance continues to transform after opening in front of an audience, and the interaction with outside observers is an essential part of the creative process. If there is an instructor they have to be part of the group as a more experienced outside eye, and they can not 'train' the performers.

Lepage's theatre embraces the idea that performers need to work with and accept transformation, change and the unknown rather than avoid them. Performers play rather than act. They are engaged in games and spontaneous interactions, not in the creation of 'serious' art. The transformation of the material depends on a number of factors (work environment, time-frame, culture and venue), but most of all on the individualities of the actor-authors within the group. The performers must be willing to write their own text, improvise for long hours and change everything at the last moment. Often the group devises hours of material through playing and free improvisation, but not all of the material is used in the performance, and what is used in one phase may change and transform into something else in another.

The instructor or group leader must set up the right environment for the workshop and prepare the participants for the next session. Enough time should be allowed between each workshop for actors to prepare their personal material. This process is about the participants' ability to do performance-writing. Although the exercises within the workshop can be done in any order that is suitable for individuals, it is essential that the next phase organically develops from the previous one. All the exercises explored here can also be seen as games where actors discover material for their performance through playfulness. Lepage's performance practice does not separate training, pre-rehearsal techniques, the rehearsal process and performance in front of the audience. They are all part of the creative process.

It is helpful to repeat relevant exercises and techniques before moving on to the next session, particularly those exercises in the early stages which are intended to work on synchronicity of the body and mind. Because of the balance between personal and group involvement, these workshops are suitable for collective engagement of up to 20 participants that can work in three to four groups. The workshops require the participants to be constantly on the inside and outside of the creative process. By going through the workshops, participants not only acquire new skills but also train themselves to increase their inner focus, concentration on objects, spontaneity and physical expressiveness.

The workshop techniques are a combination of individual and group improvised actions. The process always starts from playing with personal material, and develops towards a collective group response to that material. It is important for participants to engage in the collective creative exploration in a playful and spontaneous way, where the work environment resembles a playground. However, one must always remember that this is a rehearsal process. The outcome, whatever it is, will be communicated to the audience. No particular physical gadgets (such as balls or sticks) are necessary (unless part of a personal resource), as most of the improvisations rely on the actor's imagination, physical/emotional expressiveness and the personal stimuli relevant to the participant's experience. This is a creative process that starts as a very subjective inner work, but soon becomes externalized for the whole group to share. Improvisations turn into a collective experience through brainstorming and free associations. During the work process, continuous and honest creative feedback between group members is an essential aspect of this process. The cornerstone of *The RSVP Cycles* idea of asking the audience to respond is communication – communication between group members, and later between performers and audience.

Creating equality within the group takes away the power to make decisions from one person, and effectively disbands the teacher-student relation. There is always someone on the outside that looks at the process from the point of collective ownership. Each student is an active participant and creator of their own performance. Each participant is responsible for their own material, creating scores into which they can invite others to join. Workshops could be seen as independent from each other or in progression, where one leads to another. The duration of each exercise and session is open, depending on individual factors of each participant and particularly on the size of the group. However, the creative exercises should remain within the time constraints given to the group to complete the task. Workshops will vary in length depending on the experience the participants need to gain. Lepage's rehearsals are usually eight to ten hours long. In my experience each individual workshop lasts approximately five hours.

1.1 BEFORE YOU START YOUR WORKSHOP

It is important to have a structured work environment that feels informal at the same time. The boundaries between what is rehearsed and performed are deliberately blurred. In fact, you will rehearse while you are performing, exploring in the space the score you have created or that someone else has given to you. Group talk and discussions allow you to potentially use everything that happens in a workshop as creative material. It is essential to keep an open mind – what is planned and what is accidentally discovered is equally valuable. Because improvisations can go on for a few hours, you should film the main sessions for when you are reviewing the devised material. If there is no instructor in the group, one person should be an outside eye for the duration of an exercise. Alternatively, each workshop or rehearsal can have a designated facilitator. In addition to being involved in your own improvisations, you will also observe the work of others, being on the outside of the process. It is essential that personal and collective experience converge in these presentations.

Each participant should read the following points before starting the exercises, and remember them.

- Start the workshop with warm-up exercises and physical improvisations.
- Your warm-up exercises are not separated from the rehearsals. Just as the rehearsals, they are a way of playing.
- Use an outside eye in workshops/rehearsals. Since what you create comes out of accidents and through improvisation sessions, observing each other's work is an essential part of the improvisation workshops.
- Your work environment has to be playful and stimulating. You need to have relevant personal resources for your workshop. Bring into the workshop objects you may be using to improvise and play with. Practical workshop/rehearsal sessions are always extensions of an individual period of research that happens outside of the rehearsals.
- The space where you work is a playground, a creative environment into which you have to introduce various starting reference points.
- You are the actor-author of your performance, a writer of your character and *mise-en-scène*. However, you must be ready to change everything and embrace new discoveries in the rehearsal process.
- The process starts as individual research and solo improvisations, but there is no ownership over the material. Anyone can take any material to develop their own.
- If your starting resource is a brick wall or is about breaking apart and coming together, you will start from a personal reference point

relevant to this starting resource. How does this connect to the group's starting resource?

- Individually discovered material will be developed in a workshop. Input from other members will start changing and shaping your work which has to be open for collective playing.
- Connections and links will appear throughout the process. You may find what others are doing to be stimulating, and will use it to extend your improvisation or even as your own material.
- What is planned and what is accidental have the same value and relevance for the creative process; therefore, you must keep an open mind and be flexible to change.

2 THE BODY

The essential elements for this session are the actor's spine, creative imagination and the relation between the body and the external environment. The main focus of this session is the physical and mental connection between your body and your environment. The aim is to explore ways in which the participant/actor can use their physicality and the immediate environment in order to spiritually and mentally connect with it. This session can be done as part of a creative process, but it can also serve as a warm-up before each session. You may use warm-up exercises you are already familiar with. You need to work in a very open and relaxed atmosphere, where the group is free to play and initiate ideas. It is important that everyone is focused and maximally engaged with their creative process.

2.1 WARM-UPS

Note: As with any other practical workshops, you must warm-up first. Long improvisations and physical activities require your mental and physical focus. The main purpose of this exercise is to relax and gain inner focus by imagining your body and inner flow of energy.

You have to centre your mental energy, becoming aware of the various parts of your body. Stand in the space. Make sure that you are centred, and that your body is balanced and relaxed. You may use a number of exercises for balancing and warming-up, but ensure that you work downwards along your spine. In this exercise you are working vertically with your body.

The relaxing exercise suggested here works along your spine, and involves four segments of your body – head, shoulders, pelvic area and knees.

- Walk in the space, shaking various parts of your body.
- Find a spot in the space where you can stand. Focus on your body and internalize the image of the flow of blood through your body. Follow the journey of one blood cell circulating through you. Breathe by expanding your diaphragm. Using all of your lung capacity, let the air out through your mouth.
- Find a point of balance. Imagine that there is a pole going through your body connecting it with the ceiling. Extend your body upwards. Place your legs in line with your shoulders, slightly apart. Each leg should be in line with the corresponding shoulder. Move back and forward and from side to side, finding out at what point you are in your natural place, at your centre. You should find this as you are passing through the middle. Once at your centre, you should be completely relaxed and very flexible, so that if slightly pushed your body would take in the movement and follow it, without resistance or self-control.
- Imagine that your head is being pulled upward towards the ceiling by a balloon, extending your body vertically. Keeping both feet on the ground, pull yourself upwards as much as possible.
- Imagine that only your hands (wrists) are tied to the balloons and lift them. Then lift your elbows until both of your arms are high in the air, being pulled upwards. Your whole body is extended vertically as if you are just about to start flying. You are completely supported by balloons, literally standing on your toes.
- Slowly, one by one the balloons burst and you drop the part of the arm that has lost support until you are back to your natural position. Repeat this, with all the balloons bursting at the same time, causing the arms and upper torso to drop (without reaching the ground).
- Synchronize the extension and suppression with the flow of air so that when you suppress you let the air out through your mouth. This letting of the air out could be extended to making sounds.
- Stand still and centre yourself. After you have aligned head and body with your spine, move your head from left to right and vice versa.

Do not move any other part of your body. You should not move your neck, just your head by moving the lower part that sits on top of your spine. It is important that you feel the small movements that come from that point where your head meets the spine. Repeat this movement for about one minute.

- Take the movement to your shoulders without moving any other part of your body. Play with each shoulder individually, and simultaneously pull them up until they touch your ears and then push them down as much as you can. (Try to pull them so they can touch your ears and drop down abruptly.) Keep this movement going until you can fully imagine the inner flow of energy through your shoulders, as if it was a ball travelling from one shoulder to another.

- Extend the movement to your pelvic area, by just moving the pelvic area of your body. Start moving backwards and forwards and from side to side. Make sure you only move the pelvic area and not the whole body. Movements should be generated from the hips; no other part of your body is controlling that movement. Keep the inner focus and imagine your pelvic area as being independent from the rest of your body. Stop each time you reach the centre, before extending the pelvic movement in any of the four directions. Feel the movement of your spine as your pelvic area goes though this motion. You may extend this movement to clockwise and then anti-clockwise.

- Finally, extend the movement to your knees, moving them in a circle. The movement is only generated by your knees; no other part of your body should be part of it. Your legs should be together for this session, and make sure that the knees are 'unlocked' and soft.

2.2 IMAGINARY POLE

- Walk in the space until you find a spot where you feel comfortable.
- Stand straight and centre yourself. Imagine a vertical pole going through your body. It connects you from the ground to the ceiling. While the vertical pole goes through your body locking it in one spot, you are free to move other parts of the body in the opposite direction, as long as that part of your body remains connected to the imaginary pole. Different parts of the body are autonomous

and go in different directions – i.e. the head moves backwards, one arm pulls you to the left, and you take a step forward.

- Your body parts are free to move while you are not. See how this new movement makes you feel. Keep exploring different movements while keeping the inner focus on your spine and the pole that goes through you. What does your body say to you about the physical position you are in?
- Example: Imagine the vertical pole running through your body through your spine. Step forward with your left leg and flex your knee. Lean your upper torso backwards keeping your spine straight and shoulders back. Come back to the centre. Repeat the same movement with your right leg.

2.3 BODY SCULPTURING (Figure 4.1)

Note: The same principle applies in this exercise as in exercise 2.2.

- Find a spot in the space and centre yourself.
- Let a physical movement by one part of your body (arms or shoulders) take control over your whole body. Extend the movement while connected to the pole by any other part of your body, which remains fixed for this movement.
- Play with different movements of your head, shoulders and arms, and let them lead you. Create different images (sculptures). Keep the image of the vertical pole running through the centre while one part of your body is connected to it and to your starting spot in space.
- You can also imagine that your spine is this vertical pole and keep exploring different movements by separating the upper and lower torso. Go down on the floor and move as you would around a pole. You can move in various directions as long as one part of your body remains connected to the vertical pole.
- Imagine your body is suspended in the air or floating in water, reaching for something, as being very big or small. You may extend this exercise to focus on various emotions generated by the physical expression and use this to play with, expanding and building the next movement out of those emotions.
- Example: Lead your body by initiating movement from your head or your shoulders to one side and explore different movements so that your body extends in different directions.

Figure 4.1 Body sculpturing (exercise 2.3). Photo by Aleksandar Dundjerović.

2.4 SCULPTURE DANCE

Note: Similarly to previous exercises you are to explore physical expression, but now you will be moving throughout the space. Explore the physical quality of each movement.

- Start walking in the space. Let different parts of you body lead the movement – shoulders, knees, pelvis, upper torso, etc. Play with the rhythm. Make the movements big, extend them and make them small, make them fast and slow.
- Give yourself tasks and see how your body responds in regards to the vertical pole. You are listening, reaching out to get something, you do not understand what is being said to you, you are critical of something. The task is to find a physical image for it and to be aware of the physical body expression, as if you are observing yourself from the outside.
- Using mirrors could be very helpful in this exercise. If there is no mirror (and even if there is one) you may use another member of the group to observe you and to do your image so you can see it. You will then do the same for them.

It is important in this exercise to keep the image of your body and to remember what emotional response particular movements generate in you. Ask yourself how you feel when you do a particular movement. What is the inner image that you have? What kind of image do you project? How do specific movements affect your feelings? What emotions arise from particular physical expressions?

This exercise can also be done by exploring different physical states of your character's emotions. Explore how your character would move. How is this physical expression relevant to him/her? What does the movement suggest about him/her? How do you feel while you are doing this? The character you are devising is you in a given situation or your alter-ego, which is you but under completely different circumstances. In creating a character you can imagine someone you know, and take on their physical expression and way of behaving (thinking).

2.5 CONTACT WITH THE FLOOR – HORIZONTALITY

Note: Once you have set your verticality, you must work on the horizontal connection between your body and the space. In this exercise you will use your body horizontally, exploring movement throughout the space by using the floor surface.

- Centre yourself. Drop down on the floor. Lie down on your back with your legs extended and slightly parted, with hands next to your body. Let your body sink into the floor, taking all the pressure away from your body and into the floor. Feel your legs, pelvic area, torso, shoulders and head press against the floor.
- Slowly turn on one side. Feel the pressure move on your stomach. Once you have established a contact between the floor and various parts of your body, start moving by using the floor as a pressure point.
- Press your body against the floor and move horizontally from stillness to stretching and rolling. Move horizontally on the floor by constantly keeping a pressure point where your body is in contact with the floor. Make sure that you release the physical pressure on to the floor.

2.6 PHYSICAL CONTACT WITH PARTNER

Note: As in exercise 2.5, where you used the floor, this exercise requires you to have a constant physical contact with your partner, and to use that physical contact as a starting point for the development of a movement improvisation.

- Get into pairs and use your partner as a point of support for movement, keeping your body in continuous motion by establishing contact or pressure with some part of your partner's body (elbow, hand, knee, back, etc). You have to provide support for each other's movement.
- Through your movement improvisation, resume various images in which your position complements your partner's physical expression.
- Example a) Stand facing each other at arm's length. Extend to do a handshake. Hold your partner's hand and lean backwards using the support of your partner's weight. The point of pressure has to be on your hands.
- Example b) Stand back-to-back. Lean on your partner's back. You partner rolls on one side of you, keeping contact by pressing against your shoulder. Take your partner's hand, lean backwards and squat.

Find the best way for the movement by keeping a point of contact with some part of your partner's body that you use as support.

2.7 MOVING IMAGE

- Three groups of two will do their movement improvisation, while others observe. Do an improvisation from exercise 2.6 in a slow motion, clearly separating each new contact movement.
- If you are observing this, choose to join in the group where you can complement the contact improvisation by positioning your body in response to the existing physical image.
- Example: If two partners are as in exercise 2.3, using a handshake as a support, you can use their extended arms as a support for your back, using them as a point of contact. If they are leaning on each other you can use the arch created by their bodies to connect and complete the movement.

2.8 ENERGY BALL (Figures 4.2, 4.3, 4.4)

Note: This exercise emphasizes slow-motion routine, keeping your spine straight, following the natural movement of the body combined with breathing. Throughout the physical movement you may imagine various situations in which your body is engaged.

- Walk around the space until you find a spot where you feel comfortable to focus on your inner self. Stand straight and relaxed as in exercise 2.1.
- Imagine that there is an energy ball (not a physical ball, but rather more like a force field) that you move around or pass and receive. The rhythm of the movements should be synchronized with your breathing. Each exercise starts from stillness, from being centred and by breathing in and out before the movement is generated.
- Example a) Stand with your arms relaxed next to your body. Imagine that you are holding the energy ball in your hands. Slowly start lifting the ball with the palms of your hands facing upward. Breathe in as you lift the ball to shoulder level. Turn the palms of your hands towards the floor and push the energy ball downwards as you breathe out.

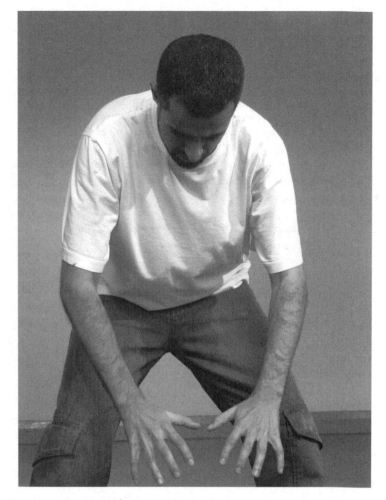

Figure 4.2 Energy ball (exercise 2.8). Photo by Aleksandar Dundjerović.

- Example b) Stand straight and take one step forward. Slowly push the energy ball away from your body with your hands, leaning forwards and breath out. Catch the energy ball in your hands, slowly moving backward and bring your hands towards your body. The movement should be done continuously as if rocking. Synchronize the movement with your breathing.

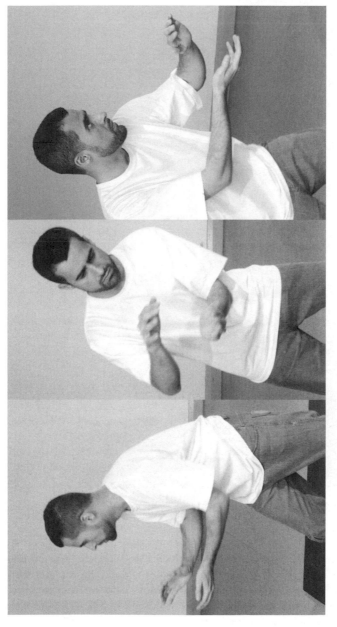

Figure 4.3 Energy ball (exercise 2.8). Photo by Aleksandar Dundjerović.

Figure 4.4 Energy ball (exercise 2.8). Photo by Aleksandar Dundjerović.

- Example c) Stand straight with your legs apart. Keep your imaginary energy ball in front of your torso. Move the ball and torso from left to right, with one palm on top of the ball and the other on the bottom. Reverse and move from right to left. The movement is generated from side to side.

- You may combine any of the forward movements with the lateral movements. Make sure that each movement gradually flows into another.

2.9 PASSING THE ENERGY BALL

Note: This exercise can have many different versions with the group passing movements, imaginary objects, sounds, claps, even lines from the text. The key elements in this exercise are the connection, rhythm and specific level of energy that are achieved while passing on the imaginary energy ball.

- One person starts by clapping their hands and then passing this clap to someone else in the circle by looking and pointing at them.
- The other person receives the clap by repeating it in the same way as it was sent, and then claps again in their own rhythm pointing to another person in the circle and passing the clap to them.
- You must respond in the same way you received the clap. You can do one clap, two claps, a few short claps, a combination of the above, etc. You must keep the rhythm and not loose the connection with your partner.
- This exercise can be repeated until there is a flow of movement between members and clear synchronicity between their movements.
- This could be even further extended to a clapping dance routine, where different rhythms are played.
- The way the clap is passed on can reflect the energy in different ways – it can be a very elegant move, a symbolic gesture or a movement sequence.

2.10 PASSING WORDS AS AN ENERGY BALL

Note: This exercise can follow from exercise 2.9 by replacing claps with sound, adding gibberish language or even existing lines from a text. The purpose of the exercises is to enhance the connection between sound/ text, movement and the group that makes your immediate environment. The passing of words can develop into a short exchange.

- The group needs to stand in a circle. Every student/participant has one letter. A looks at B and passes a ball with gibberish language as sounds implying action (accusation, seduction, questioning, etc).

- B responds to A by catching the ball, repeating the sound and action, and then transforming what was passed in gibberish into another sound and action, and passing it to C.
- C responds to B and transforms this into another verbal expression using gibberish language and passes it to D.
- The exercise goes on until everybody in the circle has had a chance to pass and receive the energy through gibberish language.
- You may play with size of the ball (small, big, beach, football, etc.) as you are passing it around.
- In the next round this can be done using a simple text. A uses the text energetically as an accusation: 'The day is bright, not one cloud in sight' and passes it to B. B responds by repeating the same text but implying a different subtext (dismisses accusation) and passing it to C.
- In the next round of this exercise you can use questions and pass them as an energy ball. A can ask a question of B: 'Do you want to go out on a date?' or 'What book are you reading?', saying it fast and intensely while passing the energy ball to B.
- B can answer either by accepting or blocking: 'Yes, I will text you my number so you can call me.' B must respond using the same energy that was received.

3 THE SPACE

3.1 THE CHASE

Note: This is a chasing game that requires high awareness and free movement throughout the space. It is important to be fully aware of the outside space, your immediate space and those who are around you.

- Establish the boundaries within which it is allowed to run and escape.
- Once you have established the outside space you need to 'see' the small circle around your body, about 50cm from your body.
- One person starts the game by chasing others – the aim is to capture them by touching their inner circle with their hand. If you are touched you have to leave the game. If you call the name of any

other member in the group before you are touched you stay in the game, and the person whose name you called out has to be the one chasing. The person chasing must keep their hands next to their body, they cannot extend them or fake a movement. Only once they are ready to touch a person can they can move their hands.

- If you are touched before you call out another name, or you call out a wrong name (i.e. the name of someone who is not in the group), you go out of the circle/space and stand as a new mark for the boundaries of the circle/space.
- If someone runs outside the boundaries, they will be out of the game. As more participants are out they join to form new boundaries, thus narrowing the space/circle and restricting movement.
- The game ends when only two participants are left in the space.

3.2. THE BUBBLE (Figure 4.5)

Note: The aim of this exercise is to create awareness of the inner and immediate space. Each participant should imagine that there is a bubble around their body. You are physically inside this bubble, invisible to others. The bubble becomes your skin, it is outside. All of your physical expression-emotion is on the inside, taking over all of the space inside the bubble.

- Walk around the space – stretch, loosen and tense your body. Move around the space in any direction. Move faster, slower, jump up or crawl.
- Once you are inside the bubble, think of an emotion and find a space in the room to physicalize this feeling within your own body. You are invisible to the others.
- Move in any way imaginable, repeat your movements and explore the physical expression of your emotion. You are protected by your bubble.
- Keep walking in the space. You remain invisible inside your bubble. Change the rhythm. Do a very fast and exaggerated movement. Create physical expression by using all parts of your body – head, neck, upper body and knees, and all the levels in the space inside of the bubble.
- Move faster, slower, make this emotion bigger, and exaggerated. Freeze.

Figure 4.5 The bubble (exercise 3.2). Photo by Aleksandar Dundjerović.

- In whatever position you find yourself in, play out the pattern of your movements in your head, see it with your mental eye.
- While remaining still in your position, visualize the way in which your body moved and remember what you were feeling. Select the key physical expressions that relate to your feeling.

- Once you complete the mental journey, begin moving inside your bubble, playing with your selected physical movements, exploring them, making them bigger or smaller. Allow them to take over your body or centralize them in one part of your body.
- The instructor or an outside eye will ask you to drop the bubble. Completely relax on the floor.
- Example: You feel pain in your body. It began with a feeling in your mind and as you started to walk around the space it caused your body to be in pain. Each new instruction, such as faster or slower, raised a different set of problems for the body in pain. The pain morphed and transgressed through fast, slow, bigger and still. Slow movements were controlled and faster movements became jagged, sharp and uncomfortable. The Freeze made you internalize the physicality of this feeling in your mind. As your action got bigger the pain increasingly took over your body.

In a brainstorming session, discuss how this movement affected your emotions. Did the mental image have a physical expression? Did it take over your body until all of your being was enveloped within this feeling? How did you make the transition from the inside to the outside of the bubble? What feelings did it expose?

3.3 OUTSIDE CIRCLE

- Step out from your bubble into the outer space. Define your circle and the space where you will focus on your action. You are to select one of the physical actions you had been doing inside your bubble which sums up your emotion. You are to repeat this action, play with it, and develop it into a physical expression.
- The next task is to share the found physical expression with the rest of the group. Each performer is to present their actions as they were working on them in the space, aware that they are performing for others who are observing. Communicate your feelings to those who are observing you.

Example: Your emotion is pain in your stomach. Your action starts with a cramping of the stomach, curling up, and then you move your left arm upwards twisting diagonally into the air in attempt to resist this pain. Repetition of this movement is turned into a mini dance routine.

- After each participant has shared their physical actions with the group, you will all sit in a circle for feedback.
- The instructor-facilitator provides an outside perception of the process, of the emotions and their physicalization. The participants reflect on the emotional journey that took place within their bodies. Has your relationship to your own body changed at different points? How did performing the action alter the emotion? How was it communicated differently when people were watching? In most cases, what comes out of these exercises is a difference between existing within the inner world of the bubble and outside once the action is observed by others.

3.4. PERSONALIZING SPACE

Note: In this exercise it is important to start from an empty space with one chair, and to make it personal by focusing on your inner space and the environment you imagine you are in – sitting in your favourite place or thinking what you did last Friday night, or remembering your friends from school.

- One participant sits on the chair in front of a group. There is no action given, except for looking at each other.
- The person sitting on the chair cannot do anything else except look at the group. This silent relation has to go on for approximately four to five minutes. Most likely there will be a sign of discomfort by both sides, particularly by the person sitting on the chair.
- Repeat this exercise, but this time the instructor/facilitator gives the participant an action or situation without disclosing any information to the other group members.
- Afterwards the instructor/facilitator reveals the action or situation previously instructed.

Example: your action is to remember someone who died. Think about the death or loss of someone known and loved, for example a parent, relative, close friend, a lover or a pet. See them there with you. You can use anything close to your personal experience.

- Once the exercise is over, the group discusses the difference between the two versions of the exercise. How did each person feel in response to the actions and different expressions that occupied the space? Were we watching someone from the group, or was this a fictional character? Or were we watching someone from the group acting for us? How did the space change with the inner action – was it more personalized for the performer? Did observers notice any difference between the two actions? You can discus what does it mean not to be performing, yet in the space occupied with the inner emotion.

3.5 LOCATIONS

Note: The aim of this exercise is to define location through objects. You should take objects and position them randomly in the space without thinking much about where you are placing them. This can vary from an indication of a location (bedroom, kitchen, street corner), to a combination of objects that can point to the aftermath of a dramatic event, or which are in collision with each other (round and sharp, small and big, different colours, etc.). On a more advanced level, this exercise can be done as an installation organized around an event that is thematically linked to a location.

- Each participant can take an object that they have with them (keys, umbrella, mobile phone, coat, bottle of water, bag, books, etc. . . .) or even an object found in the room or nearby (chair, table, wooden box, etc.). The task is to make a personal space by using the objects.
- Once everyone has placed their object in the space as relevant to their image and in relation to what is already in the space, the group observes the installation
- Try to tell a story or suggest an event by using the objects that outline the space. Play with contradictions – small objects in a large space, white sheet with red spots, the dark with one source of light, etc.
- Example: If there is a chair with a bottle of water next to it or on top of it, sit on the chair and drink from the bottle. If there is a table, sit and order food, or hide under the table.
- Upon completion of the task the group will discuss the exercise. The discussion should follow an analysis of what was intended and how it was communicated to the observers.

3.6 MOVING SPACE (Figure 4.6)

Note: This exercise aims to create a dramatic space by positioning yourself and the chosen objects in such a way that they are in a kinetic process – moving or with the possibility to move, suggesting possible change. Similarly to exercise 3.5, you are to interact with objects to create the space.

- Find your space and bring in any found objects.
- You may also interact with fixed elements in the space such as walls, rails or curtains. Look for anything that can allow movement and change of the space by interacting with your body.
- Use the objects on stage in such a way that you interact with them in a kinetic way.
- Avoid stillness and stability and look for transitions between two positions and possibilities for change.

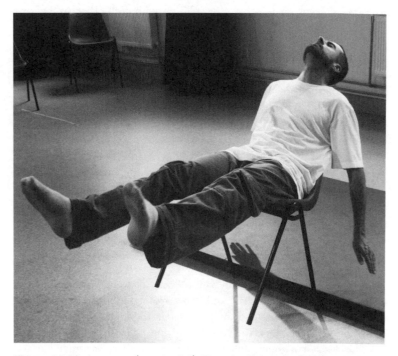

Figure 4.6 Moving space (exercise 3.6). Photo by Aleksandar Dundjerović.

Example: Sit on a chair and rock backwards so that at any point you may fall backwards. You are in between a vertical and possibly a horizontal position (if you fall off the chair). Put a pen on the back of a chair so that it balances but could also drop at any point. Lean against the wall in a way that it provides the main support for your body but not your legs.

You may extend this into a small improvisation. In groups of three, create dynamic visual images by making a live tableau that includes the possibility of movement. Use each other to play on these dynamics.

3.7 EYE CONTACT (DRAMATURGY OF SPACE)

Note: The group splits into Group P (performers) and Group O (observers). Group P uses the full space while Group O observes.

- Group P walks in the space and each participant finds a spot where to stop. You should not establish eye or physical contact with anyone else in the space. Your aim is to be as removed as possible from everyone else in the group, while keeping your inner focus. However, you should be aware of the presence of others by seeing their total body picture without looking at their eyes.
- One person (A) starts the game by establishing eye contact with someone else (B), either by walking directly to them or by physically indicating and looking in their direction until eye contact is established. The participants are to choose how they are to move, slowly or fast, with tension or rushed. B can either accept the contact and respond by looking back at A, or reject it by looking away from A or trying to establish contact with someone else in the space (C). If B accepts the contact with A, then A has to look for another person to establish contact with, until they are rejected, at which point the participant who rejected them starts the movement towards a new person in the space.
- Once all participants from group P have had their turn the groups change. The group observing is looking for images and spatial relationships between the characters, tensions that emerge from the spatial distance and the engagement that results from this game in order to feedback to those performing.
- The feedback session takes place once both groups, P and O, have played.

4 THE OBJECTS

As observed in chapter two, an important aspect of Lepage's workshops involves improvising with objects. It is through this playing that performance material is spontaneously discovered. As with other improvisation sessions, it is very important to be in the moment – to listen, be alert and focused on the situation. This session relates to the resources part of *The RSVP Cycles*, and aims to develop creative interaction between performer and objects.

4.1 IMAGINARY OBJECT

Note: In this exercise your focus is on an object which you see in your mind. It is about imagination and the ability to connect with others in the group, through physical action without using words. Although your focus is on one object, you will have to imagine yourself in an event (situation) which includes the object.

- The group forms a circle. Each participant imagines one object.
- Someone starts by playing with an imaginary object.
- Interact with the object so that it is clear from your physical actions what it is and what your relationship with it is. You can not use words.
- Pass the imaginary object to the person next to you.
- You receive the object for what you believe it is; change it into the object you had imagined, and interact with it before you pass it on to the next person.
- Once the round is completed the group has to feedback on who had what object and whether it was clear or not to others what each individual's object was.
- In the next round, start passing on the imaginary object in the same way as you did with the energy ball by throwing it to anyone in the circle.
- Once you receive the object, interact with it and then change it into an object that is associated with the one you have received before throwing it to another person.

Example: Clearly establish the object you are using. Set up a situation – you are looking for your front door keys. You do not know where they are. Once you find them you have to look for a key hole, but you are a bit drunk or it is dark so you cannot see it. You get angry and throw the keys away, in the direction of another member in the group who will take the keys and transform them into a pen to write a letter. They are not sure how to start the letter so they throw the pen to another person, who then uses it as a different object as part of a new situation.

In the next round try to connect objects through association, i.e. if you receive keys you may associate them with money, a lost piece of paper, or a mobile phone you cannot unlock.

4.2 TRANSFORMING REAL OBJECTS

Note: In this exercise you have to spontaneously respond to given indications by improvising with a physical object creating a new object and situation. Begin by taking a physical object that is found in the space (bottle of water, scarf, book, etc.).

- Someone starts by playing with a physical object.
- Pass the object to another person by calling out what this object will be now, transforming the way it is used with each exchange.
- Interact with the object, changing its meaning with your action. In other words, it is what you do with it, not what it is, that counts.

Example: The group stands in a circle. One participant takes a bottle of water and drinks from it. Once finished they throw the bottle of water to someone else in the group and call out 'bomb'. The person receiving the 'bomb' has to respond to this object, and must interact with it until they pass it on to another participant, calling out 'dog'. This person receives the starting physical object as a 'dog', interacting with it until they pass it on to the next person, calling out 'snow ball'.

4.3 RANDOM OBJECTS

Note: This exercise is about taking randomly found objects and turning them into an individual resource/object that has a personal connection with you.

- Separate into subgroups of four to five participants.
- Each subgroup is to take three objects, without much thinking, from any number of objects found accidentally in the space. Whatever is closer must be taken without any thinking. If there is a problem finding objects in the space, the group may look outside of the space, or the instructor may allow participants to take objects out of a box.
- Remember the objects mean whatever you establish in your interaction with them.
- Use the object's opposite characteristics, their negative implication or contradictions.
- You can also free-associate found objects.
- You have twenty minutes to come up with a three-minute score. Use your time to explore the objects, play with them or 'write'. Do not try out or practise the final outcome.

Example: The objects that you may use can be randomly selected, from objects that are in the room to your personal objects. For example, your group can be instructed to use a curtain, a paper cup, a necklace, a shoe, a chair, a door. As you begin playing you must establish a relation with the objects by engaging with them. You will start improvising with them. You can become chained to the chair, imprisoned by it so that wherever you move the chair moves, or you are imprisoned by your love of the chair so you move when the chair moves. You could use the cup to drink but you can also drown in the cup. Although you are trying to travel you have only one shoe. You go inside the chair, you can see through the gap but you are still behind it. You lift it up and try to separate it from yourself but it crashes behind you. You try to break free from the chair that captures you.

After you have each experimented and improvised with your objects for twenty minutes, you will all individually show to the group your étude. The observers are asked to think about what they saw and how they felt after each improvisation. What are the events being suggested by these objects? How do these accidental objects influence our personal response and the interpretation of those who observe? You can also discuss how different moments could be further developed. What is the next step that suggests itself from these accidental objects?

4.4 CONNECTING OBJECTS

Note: This exercise is similar to exercise 4.3. You are to bring your personal resource (an object or a story connected to that object) – something you find inspiring and interesting, and with which you could establish a personal connection.

- As in exercise 4.3, each member will present their object and the story connected to the object to the group.
- Each participant is to find their own reference point to the presented objects/stories.
- At the end of the presentations each member of the group will nominate the five objects/stories that were the most relevant to them.
- Those objects/stories that receive the most votes will be selected to stay as resources.
- The group is to be divided into subgroups of a maximum of five participants.
- Each group is to use all five chosen objects/stories and look for connections between them to improvise a short scene, up to three minutes long.

4.5 PERSONAL OBJECTS

Note: For this exercise you are to bring your personal resource, an object that is relevant to you. In preparation for this exercise each participant has to explore the objects, not prepare a performance or an event, and go through their qualities considering what emotions are attached to each object to bring them out. It is important to allow time between two workshops in order to have enough time to find the objects.

- Each participant should bring one physical object. This can include photos, artwork, sounds, a poem, a teddy bear or anything that is pertinent to you in some personal way, with a clear emotionally relevant story behind it.
- The group has to sit in a circle, with enough space in between each participant so that all objects can be placed in front of them. Everything has to be visible to everyone in the group.

- Each participant will tell their story about their personal object. Explain why this object is a personal resource, what is significant about this object, why this object is relevant to you.
- Observers are to carefully listen to each story, while looking for ways in which the objects/stories connect to their own experience.
- After this explanation by each member of the group, everybody will offer their own connection with the other participants object.

Example: if you have brought a letter or a photo, another participant may say what association they have with that letter or what they see in the photo and how they interpret it. How does your emotional resource (story behind the letter) relate to the other participant's experience? Everybody in the group explains their relation to each other's resource.

- Once this is completed the next round is to associate ideas connected to the physical resource introduced by the person next to you.
- The round is to provide antonyms for the introduced objects or expressed words/ideas. Opposites are a very important way of exploring resources.

Example: If love is the association for the object 'letter', then hate or passion can be its opposition. Variations of this exercise can be a collective storytelling. At any point, each association or opposition can be used as a starting point to tell a group story so that each person in the group can build on what the previous participant says.

This exercise can also be done with a random object relevant to the present time. It can be either something that is accidentally discovered or is relevant to your life in the last few hours. This can range from something you have found on the street or an object belonging to someone you have just accidentally met.

4.6 THE HIDDEN OBJECT

Note: There are different variations of this exercise, but the most important aspect of the exercise is to hide objects and then take them randomly without any pre-conceived planning.

- Separate the group into pairs, and in each pair decide who is person A and B.

- A puts his hand in a box (if there is no box, use a bag or behind the curtains or under a table) to search for an object.
- B prompts A by asking questions, helping and guiding while A searches through the hidden objects.
- One object leads to the discovery of another one, as if on a journey, which can be developed through associated images.
- Once A has finished exploring and B can no longer provoke A to search, switch sides so that B is now searching for a hidden object.

Example: A puts his hand inside a box.

B: What did you find?
A: I found something furry.
B: Is it moving?
A: No, it is still and cold.
B: Throw it away and go to the left, what is there?
A: It feels like a big wet sponge.
B: If you squeeze it what do you feel?
A: My hand is wet and if I squeeze more it is going through my fingers.

4.7 THE MAGIC BOX

Note: This exercise develops in a similar way to exercise 4.4, and it can be also used to discover objects that can be associated with the starting resource of the devising process.

- You may use a real or an imaginary box to symbolically search for objects.
- In groups of three, take turns to search inside the box (your hand should be inside the box while you are searching) for objects that are associated to the given starting resource. Each member will find something that is relevant to the starting resource.
- The group will continue with the improvisation until they know everything about this resource.

Example: Your starting resource is Amsterdam (but it can be anything – a character, location, event, etc.). Each participant comes up with something related to this place as objects that have been found in the box (flowers, a light bulb, a flat bicycle tyre, condoms, needles). You can even invent characters that live in Amsterdam or objects belonging to these characters. It is not important to be factual, but to play with objects that are somehow connected to Amsterdam through you.

4.8 CONFLICTING OBJECTS

Note: This exercise can also be part of the group improvisation section of the devising process.

- The group divides into pairs and each pair assigns who is person A and B.
- A and B choose one object (chair, table, wallet, etc.) and set up a conflicting situation creating a given circumstance (who, why, what, how, where, when) based on that object.
- It is important to set up obstacles for the tasks and objectives of each character.
- The conflicting theme can be relevant in some way to the group's chosen starting resource.
- The starting object has to be at the centre of the conflict for the improvised scene.

Example: If the group decides that the key resource/object is a bench in a park and you are improvising around various events that took place in the park, then the conflicting situation has to include two characters that need the bench for different objectives that are not compatible, such as A wants to sleep on the bench but B wants to sit down to rest a hurting leg, or A wants to read a book but B wants to talk.

5 THE SCORES

In this devising process, space is equal to score (performers' interaction with resources in the space). This session relates to the scores part of *The RSVP Cycles*. The actor-creator of scores is a writer in the space. Scores are small improvised scenes that are not connected to any narrative, but can be rearranged and edited depending on the images and dramaturgically interesting material they produce. The scores are not about remembering what has been rehearsed; they are rather a way of capturing a process annotating movement/action through space.

5.1 SCORE SHEET (Figure 4.7)

Note: This exercise uses a blank piece of paper that will become a score containing information about a future improvised scene. The aim is that each participant performs their individual improvisations based on the score sheets given to them by other members. Depending on the level of experience, the instructor may have to help to set up a score in the space.

- At the top of the paper write a theme or a starting resource. This is usually one or two words pointing to the conflict or problem that you are individually engaging in.
- Follow this by indicating the resources – a list of all elements used in the score from movement to sound and physical objects.
- Draw the stage space indicating starting lines of movement, key location when something relevant to your theme is discovered, and the finish point. Remember that you may provide as little or as much information you think is necessary for the scene. Scores indicate process, not a finished product, therefore you do not need to indicate in detail how the scene will be done.
- The score sheet may be done before the performance, or it can be a recording of a performance that has been tried out in the space.
- Once you draw a score sheet exchange it with another participant in the group and allow the other person to perform it as if it was their own improvisation.
- Each person will appropriate the given score as if it is their own. Once the score has been explained and the participant is familiar with the score sheet, they will do the improvisation in front of the

Figure 4.7 Improvisations based on score sheet (exercise 5.1). Photo by Rodrigo Garcez.

observing class without any rehearsal. Remember your focus is on the score not on performance. You are exploring a process; you are not creating a product.

- The group will feed back the most valuable actions and images in the score.

Example: The first line in your score sheet is the theme. The theme for the score can be betrayal or escape, life coming out of death, breaking apart, coming out or running away. The theme can also be a starting resource such as a pool of water, mirrors, a card game or a mobile phone. In other words, the starting point is anything you can establish a connection and personal engagement with. The second line in your score sheet is the list of resources that you are going to use in your score. For example, for the theme of escape you should list all the actions that take place in your score, including all the objects. This may be listening, breathing heavily, crawling, running, glass of water, chair, opened book, a clapping sound, text: 'To be or not to be, that is the question?', etc. In other words, anything can be used as a resource that will be part of the performers' playfulness. The third section in the score sheet is the drawing of your score.

5.2 GROUP SCORE

Note: This exercise follows on from the previous one. In this exercise we are looking for a collective score as a common starting point that comes out of the individual score sheets.

- Set the group the task of bringing together a new score on a theme that has resulted from the individual scores, and that is concrete and relevant to all the presented scores.
- You may use the starting questions to help you begin the association process. How do I do this? What is it like to do that? When did I start doing this? Do I remember a moment in my life when I was doing this? What happened, can I remember it?
- Participants should go away and research.
- For the next workshop, each participant should bring their own scores – a set of actions in the space that are associated to the starting reference point. The score has to include a set of resources written on a paper that will be given to another participant to perform.

Example: Let's say that the ideas initiated in the previous feedback pointed to 'going on a journey' or 'moving through space' or 'how to fly'. Use the questions individually or have an instructor to side coach you.

- How do I get from here to there?
- How do I move in this space?
- How would I like to move?
- How do I fly?
- How do I learn to fly?

Start by listing all the resources that you find relevant to your starting point and that you want to use on a score sheet. Include all physical actions, any sound you will make, movements of your body, objects, parts of a text (if any) or even images you may want to use. The order is not important (you may use crawling, heavy breathing, a suitcase, hand clapping, a chair, listening, the words 'Hello, Hello', humming, a text, etc.). In improvisations you need to choose how to interact with these resources. Try out your score, and then reduce the list of resources to those that you actually use until you have a clear list.

5.3 EXCHANGING SCORES

Note: Performing scores is a continuous process. It is a cyclical performance that is more exploring and writing in space (improvisation on a few fixed elements), than actual performance of found and rehearsed material. As arranged at the end of the previous section, each participant must bring a score.

- The participants will get into pairs; each pair should have a person A and B.
- A and B exchange their score sheets and explain to each other the essential resources in the score. A will take on B's score as if it is their own, and will interpret it by personally engaging with the resources
- A will go through the resources and explore the connection they may or may not have with the material. It is important that this is done live, in individual performance, and not pre-rehearsed in front of the whole group.
- B repeats the exercise.

- Before the run in front of the whole group starts, each participant will pick an image, a performance element or even a moment from each improvisation that they would like to use as their own.
- It is important to concentrate on the performance aspect and capture the movements that had the most impact on you.
- Once everyone has performed the group will collectively discuss what came out from each individual piece, and what was most relevant to the person observing as the key element/resource they would like to work with.

Participants who are observing the scores have to be focused to remember each individual performance; however, it is not necessary to remember them in the same order as they were performed. You will remember actions that have the most impact on you. From the previous group exercises you could select any objects and actions that you find valuable as an image.

Example: you can take the images from different scores such as the manual winding of a tape, the ripping of a magazine page, water being thrown with energy on oneself or the heavy breathing before a body collapses on stage. Each of these were part of someone else's score, but you may put them together and present them in the next workshop as a resource to improvise your next score. The link between these actions is not important, as the connections (and subsequent storyline) will be discovered through improvisations.

5.4 DISCOVERING SPACE (Figure 4.8)

Note: The idea behind this exercise is that space comes out of spontaneous playing, or as a response to starting resources or themes. From the individual scores choose the main objects/resources that dominate the space and the performers' environment. In other words, from the previous workshops select a resource-score that has relevance to all in the group and that can be used as a connecting device. Agree on an object that has special relevance and can be used by others to play with.

- Brainstorm to select one object/physical resource, from the previous improvisations, that was the most visually dominant and provocative on stage.

Figure 4.8 Discovering space (exercise 5.4). Photo by Rodrigo Garcez.

- The resource that has the most relevance to the group becomes the central resource that dominates the space. This can be anything from objects to sounds or even visual images (such as paintings or costumes).
- At the end of the brainstorming session, the group decides which was the most visually dominant and provocative spatial resource. The purpose is to find a spatial resource that can be used in the next round of improvisations as a connecting element that defines the space.
- This can also be done without using improvisations by using drawings, i.e. you can draw how you imagine or what is your personal response to a theme or starting resource from the devising session.
- In this exercise you may also use various visual elements to create a sense of space or even a spatial resource – using a flashlight or a candle in a dark space, positioning portable stage lights in different corners of the stage, or using a slide projector to play within the

frame created by the white light. How does the source of light define the space? How does the light change the objects in the space?

Example: If during the brainstorming the group decides that the most visually dominant resource was a heap of dry autumn leaves, this becomes the key spatial resource. This resource (dry autumn leaves) becomes the main part of the scores for the next round of improvisations. The group may decide that the stage will be covered in leaves and that all other scores will now be developed within this environment. Or it may become a personal point of reference used by each person as a fixed resource in their next improvisation cycle.

5.5 LOCATION

Note: Set up a conflicting situation around the chosen starting resource or theme. Decide on a location that is very familiar to everyone in the group, for example a location in a popular cultural reference point.

- Break up into pairs and decide who is A and B.
- Set up a basic conflicting situation using a location (where) and characters (who), taken from popular anecdotes, mass media or stories from popular culture, deliberately using obvious cultural or social clichés.
- Find an invented location and time for your performance that justifies the conflicting situation.
- Do not define anything else in advance.
- Do a short conflicting scene, improvising in front of the whole group.
- This exercise can last a few hours and the purpose is to freely improvise various material bringing different references into the process.

Example: If the starting theme is a language that we all understand and the chosen location is an airport environment, then we can have a number of situations – trying to get through customs without a visa (or claiming asylum); passing through a security check and having to strip everything; husband and wife breaking up in an airport VIP lounge; airhostess in a hotel room with a client; drunken/drugged pilot in a bar; terrorist training to blow up an airplane). Any starting point with its location can generate the action. For example, you may use auditioning for a part in a popular soap opera, or being in a TV studio recording a popular chat show.

5.6 WHAT IS THE STORY?

Note: It is important that participants are unaware of what event is taking place so that they can figure this out throughout the improvisation.

- Break into pairs and decide who is A and B.
- A is leading. A has to imagine a story (character and the environment this character is in) and its relation to B.
- B has to find out what the scene is about – where A is, their relationship, what is happening.
- You must relate to each other at all times as if within this situation. However, while A acts, B has to play with this and offer new material that A can respond to.
- See how far you can take this situation.
- Repeat the exercise with B leading and A discovering.
- It is very effective to do this exercise in front of a group so that the 'audience' is also discovering what the story is about while the performers have to keep it going as if they are both aware of what is going on.

Example: A suspects that B, his flatmate or roommate on a trip, has taken his jumper without asking and stained it, or A wants to bring a date over to the flat they share but wants B to leave. Through interaction B has to discover what is happening and take the situation further, offering material A can play with, accepting or rejecting it. Think of ways to take the story in different directions.

6 MONTAGE

The montage workshop corresponds to 'Valuaction' in *The RSVP Cycles*. It is an 'add on' workshop that comes once individual material has been generated in the previous sessions. The exercises in this workshop are connected and follow from one another. It is best if this session is done in one block. The main purpose is to learn how to select improvised material generated in the previous workshops and to edit it into performance.

In this devising process, montage refers to the selection of actions and objects which have the most value for the performance, either as images or as dramaturgical material. This is also an important phase in Lepage's devising process, relevant to the synthesis of generally unconnected material that was generated during the previous exploratory phases of the rehearsal process. This workshop is vital for the development of the storyline, since this type of devising generates an abundance of improvised material (sometime hours) that needs to be edited down to one or two hours of performance.

6.1 SELECTION OF ACTIONS

Note: For this exercise use someone else's actions or objects (from exercise 4.3 or 5.3) with which you could establish a personal reference. The ideal group size for this exercise is between six – eight participants. The initial group should be divided into adequate size subgroups. The main aim is to use an element from someone else's improvisation to select key moments to develop your own score. You can use any image that you like from any improvisation. It is important to play with found resources, reducing the presented performance to stimuli and finding your own reference point through someone else's material.

- Once individual improvisations are finished, use the outcomes to create your own score.
- Create a set of three physical movements or actions based on someone else's improvisation.
- Focus on the actions you believe to be the most important or provocative, and engage with them as if they were your own.
- Repeat some actions to see how they connect to you. Take them on and include them in your score. You should not repeat what someone else has done, but rather develop it and change it as relevant to you.
- Be free to play and improvise; let material take you in its own direction.
- Perform these actions in front of others in the group.
- When you observe others performing, look for what appears to be the connection between the three separate actions. Connect them in your mind. If you were to montage these independent actions into sequences, in what order would you do it? Is there a story

emerging? What action is missing to complete your story? Imagine that each of these actions constitute a segment of a story, and construct different events around them.

- Collectively brainstorm what was good and what was not, responding to the ideas that came out of the improvisation.

Example: Let's assume that you select three actions from the previous improvisations – handkerchief, praying and chair. Handkerchief – you cry and look for a handkerchief, clear your face, cover your face with the handkerchief. Praying – you kneel down, hit yourself in the back, rhythmically and then slowly you go in circles on your knees. Chair – you lie down flat on the chair and extend your hands as if you were flying, playing it as if really being suspended in the air.

6.2 SELECTION OF SCORES

Note: You are to edit the scores of different groups and select actions made of key moments – resources (images, objects, sounds/texts, actions) that you found relevant in their études. Use this as material for your score. Select a key action from each score and see how you can create a new improvisation through montage. The narrative is not important at this stage; however, it will start showing itself the longer this workshop lasts. Initially you will work individually on this exercise.

- Find a place in the space where you can establish your inner circle. It is important that everyone in the group can work simultaneously in their own personal space.
- Re-work the starting score by weaving someone else's action, which you find stimulating, into your performance. You may use your original starting point and add three – four actions picked up from other scores.
- Participants take turn to perform the new edited score in their circle while others observe. Participants have to look for what comes out of the connected actions, what themes are suggested.
- Once all the scores are performed, the group will have to sum up each presented score in one word.
- Discuss what happened in each score and what elements you could connect with and how. When you receive feedback, remember that

it is not important what you conceptually wanted to achieve. How did you relate to the observers and what they got out of it? What was the audience's response?

- It is important to remember that rehearsing has to take place in front of the group while performing. The purpose is to create in front of the group; however, you may also do the same exercise individually, exploring the images and working with objects for much longer, even an hour. It is important for the group leader or someone else from the group to observe the process.

Example: if you are editing objects and actions from the previous example, you may use a repetitive action. You could lie back across the chair, rip the magazine paper, dab water on your face, sit up exhaling loudly and then return to lie back on the chair. You may play with the rhythm – first slowly, purposefully, then speed up. Let the performance take you. Do movements harder and faster, throw water all over yourself, extend the physical movement, perform the same image without any objects, slap your face, push the score as far as you can. Once you finish, consider how far you could take this and when you felt unstable.

6.3 SELECTION OF STORY

Note: Separate the group into subgroups of between three to five participants. Each person in the subgroup is to share one event from their life. For example, an event that marked your summer break or a recent experience; it could be something from everyday life or something that had an important effect on you.

- Take turns to tell your stories. Everyone in the group should carefully listen to and remember all the stories, and should be able to re-tell them if asked to do so.
- When listening, ask yourself what you like in the event being told. Take what you find to be the most relevant as a personal reference point. What can you connect to? Is this event similar to your experience? Could you remember a similar situation?
- Once everyone is finished, the groups should mix so that each person is now part of a new subgroup with no two members of a previous group together.

- Share with others the event from the previous group which you liked the most. You have to use someone else's story. You cannot use your own story.
- Each subgroup should create their own event based on the space/object environment selected from a chosen event/story. Where and when is your event taking place? Who is involved in it? What is the location for it and how does it use the central space/object? How does location change the action and characters? Why? For whom is this done? Who leads and who follows in the main action?
- Your event does not have to follow narrative patterns; you may explore the chosen key actions that are the most relevant for each event.
- Once you have agreed on the space/object, create a short performance through the montage of the key actions from the event. Do not use more than fifteen–twenty minutes for this task.
- Show your event to the whole group.
- Change the order of the actions and see the impact this has. This is not about creating a cause–effect story but about the ability to find new connections and montage an existing story into new material.
- Show your improvisation to everybody in the group.
- This process of montage can be repeated so that in the next round the group can look for images, movement, connections and personal references that have come out of the performed events. This results in another round of improvisations.
- For this exercise you may also use a DVD camera connected to the TV or a projection screen. Each subgroup will use one camera to film their event, deciding what aspect of the event to focus on. Look at the differences between what is performed live and what is shown on the screen. You may play with different perspectives, i.e. showing the action from a personal point of view or from above. How does this change the perception of the action? How else can you use the camera to montage actions?

6.4 BRAINSTORMING

Note: This is a vital part of the process. It can take place in the editing phase but it can be there after every phase. In the same way warm-ups are to be used to start the process so that there is no separation between exercises and rehearsal, the brainstorming should be used at the end of the process. The purpose is to initiate new ideas for the next round of explorations or selections. Group discussions also allow very personal exercises to become collective, allowing space for the discussion of what makes up dramaturgical threads that will help organize the presented material. The objective is to find a common theme that connects all the different scores, that could be set up as a joint theme for the whole group to work with.

- Draw up a chart where you can compare your starting point and the themes that emerge from the presented scores. It is important to give your response as if this is your own piece. Where would you take it next or what would you want to use from it?
- Discuss the re-occurring and common themes based on what comes out from the chart sheet. What is the central image in the score? What ideas are associated? What is the story hidden behind this image? What is the ambient of the score? What is the main emotion? What style/genre is it? What music does it go with? Where is this character going? What are they doing there? What motivates them? What do they want to become?

Example: Based on the previous exercise, look for what is central in the presented scores, including Anticipation, Apprehension, Expectation, Journey, etc. What do these ideas have in common? It is important to find out the reasons behind someone's actions. Where do they want to go? What motivates them to do what they have done? What needs to be done in order for them to achieve their objectives, to go somewhere, to arrive at their destination? What is pulling them back, why are they not achieving this? Where will they arrive? Is this what they wanted? It is important to find out the obstacles and conflicts.

6.5 ALTER EGO CHARACTER

Note: These exercises are intended to help you discover your alter ego character, which will transport you inside the material.

Your alter ego is a character you are familiar with. It is similar to the concept of yourself, but in the given circumstances (who, why, what, where, when, how) of the situation you are devising. Lepage's alter ego character mirrors his own feelings at that moment in time. He is typically an artist, often a displaced person (living outside of his location, or an immigrant).

- Take someone you know and with whom you have shared experiences. Be that person by imitating their way of talking, of behaving, their way of thinking and reacting.
- Place that character in the situation you are devising and see how this character would respond and interact with their environment. Improvise a situation based on that character and create a text.
- Audio record the text, saving everything that comes out. You can draft this into a text as your monologue. What persona came out of it? Who is this person who talks through you?

A variation of this exercise can be done by drawing an alter ego character. If you have access to Photoshop you can use it to play with the images and alter the character. It is important to ask the following questions: what are they wearing, what is the body type, where do they live? What are this character's hobbies? What images does this character invoke in your mind? You may also do a collage of different images as cut-outs that relate to the qualities of this character. After you have created an image of your alter ego character, you can then proceed to make this character by finding their relevant costume and environment.

7 TEXT

This workshop uses a written text as a starting point to create the performance. The text is used as a resource in the same way as an object or personal story. It is important for the group to use segments from texts with which the whole group is familiar (*Antigone*, *Three Sisters, Faust*, *A Midsummer Night's Dream* or *Hamlet* can provide a rich starting resource).

Each dramatic text consists of a set of group events, and is made of sections or scenes. These events/scenes can be seen as scores. The narrative connects the scenes/scores either in a linear, cause-effect, circular or fragmentary way.

In devising the performance from a fixed text or a collage of texts, you bring into the text a plurality of references from your personal and your collaborators' experiences. You may want to bring into rehearsal your day-to-day experiences to aid the development of character and relationships from the text.

7.1 TEXT-BASED SCORE

Note: The idea behind this workshop is to approach text as score by taking an event (or a short scene) as an independent score with its own narrative. This approach to text is similar to a traditional director's textual analysis – breaking a play into events.

- Choose a section of a scene from a text that has a clearly recognized event and can stand on its own.
- The section must have a beginning, middle and end. The who, where and when of the scene must be easily identifiable.

Example: Break *Hamlet* Act I, Scene 1 into the following sections.

A – From Bernardo's first line: 'Who's there?' to directions *Enter Horatio and Marcellus*.

B – From *Enter Horatio and Marcellus* to the line 'Bernardo: Sit down awhile, and …'

C – From 'Bernardo: Sit down awhile, and …' to the direction *Exit Ghost*.

D – From *Exit Ghost* to the line 'Horatio: That can I …'

- Make sure that you follow the main action and the development of plot, choosing to create sections with clear events.
- Analyse the scene in a traditional way in terms of the beginning, climactic moment and end. Define what the main event in the scene is and name it.
- What is the conflict in this event? What are the given circumstances of this event?
- On the score sheet, under resources, list the following.
  - The selected verbal text (the lines you will be using). If you need to cut the lines do it. Write them down, one following another.
  - Who are the other characters in the scene?
  - What is your relation to the other characters and how is this relationship physically manifested?
  - Where and when is the scene taking place?
    How do the characters move? How do they interact? What is the distance between characters in the space?

- What are the characters doing?
- The essential objects – props in the scene or the ones you want/or need to use.
- The score starts at the beginning of the scene and finishes at the end of the scene. The climactic moment relates to when something important has happened or you have discovered something.
- Once you have created your score, exchange it with another member of the group. What do you make out of their score?

7.2 PERFORMING TEXT AS SCORE

Note: It is important to use scenes from two different texts. The text can be seen as a score with various resources. In order to understand differences, take scenes from different texts and compare them.

- Compare a scene from an open score text (with very little or no indications or even characters with lines only) with a more defined but still open score indicating just location and characters (such as in Elizabethan theatre), or with a closed score (such as realistic theatre).

Example: Open score – *Attempts on Her Life* by Martin Crimp; semi-open score – Shakespeare's *Hamlet*; semi-closed score – *Boy Gets Girls* by Rebecca Gilman; closed score such as *The Dolls House* by Henrik Ibsen. In the following exercise I suggest you use Anton Chekhov's *Three Sisters*, and *Polygraph* by Robert Lepage and Marie Brassard. *Polygraph* and *Three Sisters* are used to show the differences of texts as score and how they can act as a blueprint for performance.

Explore the style. How does the fragmented and filmic style of *Polygraph* differ from the psychologically detailed, realistic and very structured style of *Three Sisters*? Look at the main narrative and sub-narratives in *Polygraph*, particularly the collage of the small histories of the characters and the plurality of stories, and compare it to the grand text, figures and characters in the central narrative of *Three Sisters*.

- Divide into groups of about four to stage a brief scene (one clear event, not more than a page or so) from the beginning of act three of *Three Sisters*.
- Begin by breaking down and analysing the text. Look at the main action, storyline, entrances and exits of the characters. Break down

the scene into events of clear action, events which alter the action and engender conflict between characters. You may also use the pattern in creation of scores from 7.1.

- Collectively, the group must decide which flexible resources to use – space, relationships, lines, physicality, etc.
- Interact with physical objects, location and other characters, not necessarily based on what is written on the text but on how you feel, who your character in that scene is, and what comes out of it for you.
- Show the scenes to the group and brainstorm looking for what came out of it.

7.3 PERSONALISING THE TEXT

Note: To personalize the text means to put yourself and your emotions inside the text. The personal feelings are stimuli from which you will re-create and interpret the text. The idea is not to reproduce written text but to find your own 'personal text' and to create a history and justification (motivation) for the character's lines.

- Think about an immediate experience from your life, that is still fresh and had an effect on you; for example, a fleeting encounter with another person just before you came to the rehearsal. Was there a connection between you? If you had a night out, remember the interactions you had and how they make you feel now.
- Try to remember how you felt, try to feel this again. Are you still influenced by these feelings? Using the dominant emotion that is in you, approach a given scene from the text you are working with.
- Read the scene with your group and change/adapt the character(s) according to the feelings that dominated you outside the rehearsal/ class.

Example: If the experience that you brought into rehearsal is falling in love, play the scene as a love scene regardless of the playwright's indications in the text. If your experience was about being hungover and embarrassed by what might have happened while you were drunk, bring this into the interpretation of the scene and try the scene/score in this way.

7.4 TIME LIMITATIONS

Note: This exercise is important to set up the right state of mind for the creative process. It is about creating obstacles that you have to work against. By pushing yourself against time limits you enhance your creative potential and use your subconscious mind more actively.

- Depending on the scene, in groups of two, three or four choose a section of the text.
- Set up a very clear time-limit to stage it. This should be no more than twenty minutes in order to stage a three to four minute score.
- You cannot read from the text in the performance. Everything has to come from you, in the way the text is connected to yourself. It is important not to attempt to memorize the text, but work from the text as score using the lines as just another resource.
- The purpose of your twenty-minute exercise is not to rehearse, but to 'write' a score based on your reference points and the character you are doing.
- You can either use the exercise from 7.2 to establish a personal text or re-work a written scene as a score as in exercise 7.1.
- You may find that text-based scores can relate to themes you have been exploring in the previous workshops. You may look for themes that you have already discovered as a group theme in the previous exercises and want to build on.
- Once you have 'written' the text for performance (decided on and explored the key moments, actions and relationships) you will perform this without rehearsal in front of the whole group, showing your scene/score in a duration of three–four minutes.

7.5 CONNECTIONS

Note: This exercise continues from 7.4 and is about the montage of the material that has been performed. Although you are working from a text, the approach is similar to the selection process in devising a score. It is important to look for the connections that are built within a chosen scene between verbal text, images, physical action and space. This is not about the interpretation of the text or narrative but about performance; how to use performance as a resource for the next creative cycle.

- After all groups have presented the different scenes from their chosen text as their score, there is a collective brainstorm to connect resources.
- Identify the key moments in each scene. It is important to look at valuable images or ideas that may have an impact on you as an observer.
- The material presented is collective, and you may take another score or elements from it as your own.
- Once you have selected the key moments, look for the possible connecting resources that bring all the scores together. This could be the main resource as a theme, space, object, etc.

Example: Look at the scene as if you are directing it. What are the most relevant images that come out of the score? Are there any common themes? Is there any resource that appears in all the scores? Is there an image, action or movement that embodies the main theme? Take someone else's performance. What are the key moments in this performance that connect with you? What are the most relevant themes? Explore the key images that you connect with and provide your own context for them. In this new cycle you are not following the text but the performance you have seen and the starting resources that have a connection with you. Since you are essentially making a collage, this is a very energising workshop. If the emphasis is on the text or words, then by playing with them and using them in different contexts you develop this resource further. The purpose is to instinctively connect with the material by playing with it as if for the first time.

7.6 RE-LOCATING SPACE

Note: This exercise is about finding a different space from the one indicated in the stage directions for the action in the text.

- Situate your score in a space that is different from the one indicated in the text.
- Your location must alter the action in a very substantial way.
- Adapt your segment of the text based on the newly established location. Define the relevant lines for your character based on the relationship with other characters and what your objective in the scene is.

- Are there any relevant objects in the scene that you may need in the new location to help your character's objective?
- Try out the text in this new environment. How has it changed? What does this new environment add to the interpretation?

Example: In 1992 Lepage staged *A Midsummer Night's Dream* at the Olivier in London's Royal National Theatre. The huge proscenium stage was transformed into a pool of mud, effectively becoming a mud bath where the actors performed. The central object in the space was a bed that resumed various theatrical qualities and meanings based on actors' appropriations. By changing the performers' environment, Lepage altered their physical presence, the *mise-en-scène*, and the way in which the characters interact with each other. Alter the location of the fixed text of your choice. What happens if the text is played in a public toilet, shopping mall, in a war hospital, in a nightclub, during a family birthday?

CONCLUSION

There is no final destination in Lepage's devising process towards which the group works collectively. It is theatre in process that uses all the available resources (intentional and accidental) to aid the actors' authorship of performance text. Regardless of its technological and theatrical complex expression, this is fundamentally improvisation theatre that follows on a rich tradition of poor theatre with empty spaces and objects, actors as authors of their own text and a play that is shaped by the interaction with the audience. As demonstrated in a number of his solo shows, Lepage himself is a skilful performer/improviser. In the devising process, the writer, actor and director are not independent functions. Although Lepage has over time resumed this role, he is more of a facilitator and editor than a director or writer, actor in the traditional sense. Everyone involved in the process has to improvise, from the actors to the technical crew and digital engineers. It is all coming together (or not) in a live moment in front of the audience.

The audience has an important place in the performers' improvisations, and it is essential for Lepage's 'work in progress' process. The audience is introduced at the very end of the cycle in open or public rehearsals to help develop the next cycle. Regardless of whether the performance is just segments of various unconnected scores or there is actually an emerging and connecting narrative, the audience's response is an essential part of this type of devising process. Lepage explains that 'the audience is a very creative writer in the process – people don't necessarily come up afterwards and say, "I think you should do that", but they do contribute by their reactions' (Whitley, 1999, 23).

Another characteristic of Lepage's devising process is that it is made for international festivals. It is presented to festival audiences, accustomed to high-end theatre culture, whose aesthetic preferences inform his theatrical expression. Susan Bennett explains that as 'the artist works within the technical means available and within the scope of aesthetic conventions, so audiences read according to the scope and means of culturally and aesthetically constituted interpretative processes' (Bennett, 1994, 99). In turn, this 'interpretative process' informs Lepage's editing process of the existing performance material for a new cycle. Each production is rewritten through cycles while taken on tour. Lepage points out that this is 'a completely different way of directing. And it's very risky, because, of course, the first versions of our shows are sometimes full of great intent, but very clumsy' (Whitley, 1999, 23). The international auditorium profoundly influences the development of a performance.

Finally, Lepage's theatre combines multi-media performance, cinematic visual images and a plurality of arts and cultures. He mixes various media and technologies in the *mise-en-scène*. Lepage plays with cinematic images through projections of films, videos, photos, digital images, but also with simple technology like slide or overhead projectors. Parallel to improvisations with media and technology, Lepage also plays with resources that are borrowed from other cultures, particularly Oriental traditions such as Bunraku puppet, Noh theatre, Javanese shadow puppets, and Tai-Chi. These forms are not approached in their original contexts or as the result of anthropological studies, but rather as resources, as provocation, as a game, a way of telling a story or an object whose meaning can inspire performers.

Following Lepage's experience with this working practice, the devising process explained here is about the actors' ability to write and be artisans, their willingness to research and to be able to abandon found material in order to discover new ones. Theatre does not necessarily have to start from a text or words; it can start from an impression, an image or anything that provokes a personal response. It is not about intellectual engagement and expensive digital media, but about storytelling through performativity and spontaneous playing with resources (objects, space, body and technology), about being intuitive, and finding order in chaos. Lepage's way of making theatre originally started from poverty and a lack of means, yet through freedom of imagination and inventiveness a rich and powerful theatrical expression is created using simple technical means (Figure 4.9).

It is touring theatre that uses subjective material to tell epic stories; fragmenting, blurring and transforming events, recounting them as personal mythology and oral memory.

Figure 4.9 Robert Lepage's final version of *A Midsummer Night's Dream* in the Théâtre du Trident in Quebec City, 1995. A pool of water is the central location for performers actions. Photo by Daniel Mallard.

GLOSSARY

Anderson, Laurie (1947–) is an American experimental performance artist, composer, writer and musician. Anderson's performances explore multi-media (visual projections, films, graphics, sculptures, mime and electronic art) and a range of subject matters. One of the central themes in Anderson's work is that of exploring the effects of technology on human relationships and communication. She originally trained as a visual artist and learned to play the violin. She invented the tape-bow violin in 1977, which uses recorded magnetic tape. Anderson has updated and modified this device over the years. Lepage collaborated with Anderson on his solo show *The Far Side of the Moon*, composing the music.

Appia, Adolph (1862–1928) is a stage designer whose ideas and theoretical writings revolutionized theatre production in the twentieth century. His central idea was that of a total artist as a creator of the performance (theatre or opera) who unifies the functions of director and designer. Appia rejected painted two-dimensional sets for three-dimensional 'living' sets and gave dramaturgical function to lighting, believing that shade was as necessary as light to form a connection between the actor and the environment. Through controlling light intensity and colour, Appia created a new perspective of theatre space. His use of stage lighting and theatre space pioneered modern stage design. He incorporated new technologies into theatre, notably emerging electrical light.

Arcand, Denys (1941–) is Canada's most critically recognized film *auteur*. In 1986 he wrote and directed *Le Déclin de l'empire américain* (*The Decline of the American Empire*), which won the International Critics Prize at the Cannes Film Festival and was nominated for an Academy Award for Best Foreign Language Film. In 1989 his film *Jésus de Montréal* (*Jesus of Montreal*) won the same three Genie awards, plus the 'Jury Prize' at Cannes. Lepage acted in this film and often refers to his experience with Arcand as very relevant for his own filmmaking. In 2003 Arcand made *Les invasions barbares* (*The Barbarian Invasions*), which won the Best Screenplay Award at Cannes, was nominated for a Golden Globe Award as Best Foreign Language Film and won the Academy Award for Best Foreign Language Film.

Barker, Clive (1952–) Born in England, Barker is a multi-faceted author (writer of a number of short horror stories, screen and theatre plays), a visual artist, a director and an actor. He was immensely influential on contemporary visual culture with his images embodied in his writing and drawings. The book *Theatre Games* was originally published in 1988, and represents his work exploration as an actor and theatre author.

Barthes, Roland (1915–80) was a philosopher, literary critic and social theorist. His works are of major importance to contemporary intellectual and critical debates on semiotics, narratives and questions of authorship. His writing made structuralism (and post-structuralism) one of the leading twentieth-century intellectual movements.

Bausch, Pina (1940–) Bausch is one of the seminal performance figures of the twentieth century. Born in Germany, she changed the style of dance-theatre style performance that combined strong visual style, text and movement. She studied with leading German choreographer Kurt Jooss and at the prestigious Juilliard School in New York City. In 1972 she became an artistic director of Tanztheater Wuppertal Pina Bausch, one of the most provocative dance-theatre companies that regularly performs around the world. As choreographer-director her distinct *auteur* signature brings together physical and verbal expression, combining short dialogue with physical movement in a theatrical expression made of very powerful visual imagery. Her staging has been generally used as a precursor and point of comparison with Lepage's image-driven theatricality.

Bieito, Calixto (1963–) is a Spanish (Catalan) theatre director and artistic director of Teatro Romana from Barcelona. He is known for his radical interpretation of classic theatre and operas, exposing hidden sexual references and deliberately playing on them – emphasizing incest, sodomy, necrophilia and orgies within the classical text canon. Despite their controversial nature, his productions have made him one of the most in-demand directors across Europe.

Brook, Peter (1925–) is a theatre and film director, born in London. Brook's theatre directing was inspired by Edward Gordon Craig and Antonin Artaud. In 1970 he left London for Paris, where he set up the International Centre for Theatre Research. He explored intercultural theatre in search of a universal theatre language. He wrote a number of influential books on theatre practice, of which his first, *The Empty Space,* is considered one of the key readings on contemporary theatre. His 1970 production of *A Midsummer Night's Dream* was an important influence on Lepage's own staging of this text in 1992. As a director, Lepage has been often compared to Brook and seen within the context of Brook's theatricality.

Bunraku or **Ningyo** is a form of Japanese traditional puppet theatre. Founded in the seventeenth century in Osaka, it was popularized in the mid-nineteenth century. Each full-bodied puppet is operated by at least three puppeteers, who are fully visible to the audience. All puppeteers wear black hoods over their heads. Bunraku puppets range from 2½ to 4 feet or more, depending on the age of the character and the conventions that each specific troupe establishes.

Carbone 14 was a collective theatre company founded by Gilles Maheu in Montreal. (The company dissolved in 2005.) The group produced a style of physical theatre that emphasized form, image and experiment. Their very distinct expression focused on action that prevailed over text and improvisation over fixed interpretation, including in their staging special environmental and accidental circumstances. From the beginning, it excited local and international audiences and influenced performance art in Quebec. Lepage often points to Maheu as the Quebecker theatre director who had the most impact on his work.

Cirque du Soleil ('Circus of the Sun') is based in Montreal, Canada. This multi-disciplinary circus is an international entertainment empire. The company was founded in 1984 by a former street performer from Quebec City, Guy Laliberté. Originally it brought together street performance, acrobatics, juggling and dance theatre into a small-scale company that toured cities in Quebec. Over the last two decades the company has grown into a major exponent of the global entertainment industry, combining elaborate and spectacular visual and physical imagery, circus and dance theatre, and operating in five continents with an annual budget of 600 million US dollars. The budget for Lepage's directing of the show *KA* in 2004, which premiered in Las Vegas, was around 200 million US dollars.

Cocteau, Jean (1889–1963) was a French poet, artist, writer, theatre and filmmaker who pioneered multi-disciplinary creativity using a range of arts as media to express his poetic and very personal vision. Cocteau was a total author. He wrote, directed and designed his theatre and films and was particularly important in introducing Surrealism on film and in theatre. Cocteau collaborated with several well-known artists, including Igor Stravinsky, Pablo Picasso, Eric Satie and Leonde Massine. His addiction to opium affected his work. His films include the 'trilogie' that spanned most of his creative life – *Le sang d'un poète* (*The Blood of a Poet*) from 1930, *Orphée* (*Orpheus*) in 1950 and *Le testament d'Orphée* (*The Testament of Orpheus*) in 1960. Lepage credits Cocteau as one of his great teachers and inspirations, basing his solo show *The Needles and Opium* on Cocteau's life and art.

Director-author refers to the process of creating theatre where the director has the main artistic authorship over a production (as opposed to the producer, playwright or actors) and for creating the meaning of the piece. The director-author is a scenic writer who creates stage 'text', whose vision and style is made of all the production elements, equally combining the visual, the physical, technology and dialogue into one aesthetic expression for spectators.

Dodin, Lev (1944–) is a leading contemporary Russian theatre director and is artistic director of St Petersburg's Maly Drama Theatre. He has performed at major international festivals and is renowned for staging and adapting Russian classics.

Dramaturgy is the art of analysing, developing and structuring a written play, and examining all texts as possible material for theatre performance. The dramaturg is the professional who deals with creating or structuring a story that can be acted. Dramaturgy looks for a source of knowledge and examines links between form and content.

Gabriel, Peter (1950–) is a composer, musician, writer and video-maker. Widely recognized for his leading innovative music artistry, Gabriel co-founded the group Genesis when at school. After leaving Genesis in 1975, Gabriel went on to a solo career releasing 11 solo albums. April 1993 was the start of the 'Secret World Tour' and of his collaboration with Lepage, who directed the concert. The show blended Lepage's visionary style of theatre with Gabriel's personal songs, focused on relationships. Gabriel combines music and his political activism – he has been involved in a wide spectrum of human rights and environmental issues. In 2005 he gave a number of concerts as part of Live 8 events to support the 'Make Poverty History' campaign.

Halprin, Anna (1920–) is a choreographer and movement peda-gogue. In the 1950s, she was one of the western pioneers of an expressive art healing movement – using dance to cure body/soul, enhance personal expression and creativity. In 1955 she founded the groundbreaking San Francisco Dancer's Workshop and her students (Meredith Monk, Trisha Brown, Yvonne Rainer and Sally Gross, among others) revolutionized modern dance. With her husband, Lawrence Halprin, she founded *The RSVP Cycles* – a creative technique that emphasizes connections between environment/space and body/physical expression. Her recent books include *Moving Toward Life, Five Decades of Transformational Dance* and *Returning to Health With Dance, Movement and Imagery*.

I Ching: The Book of Change is the oldest Chinese text (and possibly the oldest book in the world, dating to 3000 BC). *I Ching* perceives the universe as a never-ending process of change and as part of existence. The book unfolds laws and principles that explain where we are now and where we will be in the future. It uses 64 images (hexagrams) that embody relevant meanings about a state or process to be interpreted. For *The Dragons' Trilogy*, the principles, structure and symbolical representations in *I Ching* were important for Lepage's devising and for the selection of improvised material.

Installation art mixes any media to create an intervention into a site, a chosen environment. It uses sculptural material, ranging from natural material to new media and digital technology. Taking its work outside the galleries, it establishes a relation between objects and everyday public life. Often installation is designed for a site-specific location to correlate and exist in the space for which it is created.

Intercultural implies an exchange that takes place between two or more cultures. It also refers to a cross-cultural theatre that as a phenomenon has dominated artistic theatre (and in particularly the festival theatre scene) since the late 1960s. It started taking place in a more defined way at the beginning of the twentieth century, when western theatre (as well as artists in general) started to be significantly influenced by non-western artistic concepts and philosophy. The intercultural practice can be grouped into the following categories – taking the impulse from a dominant form and regarding it as a model to be replicated by a foreign culture; keeping the original form at the centre but expanding it to take on a new set of meanings that conforms to a foreign culture; creating a new form that aims at a universal (international) language of the theatre.

Johnstone, Keith (1933–) is a theatre pedagogue who was a major influence in establishing improvisation as way of making theatre and training actors. In the 1970s he co-founded Loose Moose Theatre in Calgary (Canada) and invented Theatresports, a way of doing and teaching theatre that became a cornerstone in contemporary improvisation and stand-up comedy.

Kaprow, Allan (1927–2006) was a painter and a pioneer in establishing performance art in America. In the 1950s he developed improvised spontaneous multi-disciplinary events – 'happenings' – that involve interaction with the audience. His work aimed to integrate art and life and remove the separation between artists and audience. He was a Professor of Visual Arts at the University of California, San Diego.

Kott, Jan (1914–2001) was a Polish critic and theatre theoretician. In 1966 he moved to the US, where he taught at Yale and Berkeley. He won fame and recognition for his readings of the classics, above all Shakespeare. His books *Sketches on Shakespeare* (1961) and *Shakespeare our Contemporary* (1965) became the most widely read works of criticism at the time. The books interpret Shakespeare from an existential and political experience that was relevant to Kott's personal position at that point (and was rooted in a mid-twentieth century perspective). His writing became an important critical revision of Shakespeare and the theoretical foundation for Peter Brook's seminal production of *A Midsummer Night's Dream* in 1970.

LaLaLa Human Steps is Quebec's leading theatre dance company, combining strong physical expression with acrobatics and visual images. Started in 1980 by Edouard Lock, the company has earned international recognition by developing a unique choreographic language. The choreographic complexity consists of an alteration of balletic structures – and the intertwining of modern dance, musical and cinematic qualities, combined with a deliberate sense of perceptual distortion, encourages audiences to both reinvent and rediscover what the body can do and its physical expression.

LeCompte, Elizabeth (1944–) is a founding member of the theatre collective The Wooster Group, New York. In the 1970s she joined Richard Schechner's The Performance Group, where she developed her experimental style together with Spalding Grey (performer, deviser and theatre pedagogue). Over the last three decades the group has explored the process of performance creation through engagement with live and recorded media, eclectically bringing together film and video, sound, dance and movement with text and dialogue. LeCompte mixes classical texts with found material and actors' improvisation. The group has toured extensively around the world, particularly in Europe, Asia and Australia. Lepage's style of work and production organization has often drawn comparison with LeCompte's collective based, multi-media and eclectic directing style.

Lecoq, Jaques (1921–99) was a leading world theatre pedagogue. After studying and working in physical education and sport, he became an actor and member of the *Comediens de Grenoble*. He worked in Italy in the commedia dell'arte style for a number of years, experimenting with mask, mime and movement. Upon his return to France in 1956 he opened *L'École Internationale de Théâtre*

Jacques Lecoq, dedicated to actors' training in mime and physical theatre. The performance style emphasized interaction with the audience, an extended use of everyday space and movements, and a focus on the physical rather than the emotional side of the character. He had a major influence on a number of leading theatre practitioners who either studied with him (Theatre de Complicité) or were trained in his techniques (Robert Lepage at the Conservatoire).

La Ligue Nationale d'Improvisation (LNI) comprises improvised performance, based on sport as a comparative game. Created in 1977, the idea was to give theatre actors a forum in which to practise and perform in front of an audience a short improvised étude lasting between thirty seconds and twenty minutes. Participants form teams of six players (three men and three women). A referee randomly picks a theme card that describes a situation the participants must play. The teams have twenty seconds to conceive the situation. At the end of the match the audience votes for the best presentation.

Mise-en-scène, translated literally from the French, means 'action of putting on stage the play'. It refers to all the elements of visual style in a production and their relationship to each other. The term can also include the positioning and movement of actors on the set, which is called blocking or staging. When applied to the cinema, *mise-en-scène* refers to everything that appears before the camera and its arrangement – sets, props, actors, costumes and lighting.

Mnouchkine, Ariane (1939–) founded the Parisian experimental company Théâtre du Soleil in 1964. She is committed to people-theatre, and uses performance as a tool for socialist political action. She and her company use various techniques in developing performance (from commedia dell'arte to Asian rituals), borrowing from other ancient cultures, particularly Oriental traditions. Théâtre du Soleil's productions are often performed in found spaces like barns or gymnasiums, because Mnouchkine does not like being confined to a typical stage. Mnouchkine's long-term collaborator is the cultural theorist and writer Hélène Cixous.

New baroque refers to an artistic style that has similarities to the baroque style but is from a contemporary period. It has the most applicability in architecture, but it can also relate to decorative arts as well as writing and theatre performance. Revival of baroque is particularly relevant to Quebec's architecture.

Noh (or **Nōgaku**) is a traditional Japanese musical drama, consisting of slow symbolic movement, music and chanting that has been performed since the fourteenth century. As an artistic form, Noh was established and promoted by shogun and ruler of Japan, Ashikaga Yoshimitsu, a friend of the first Noh performers Kanami Kiyotsugu and his son Zeami Motokiyo. Together with the closely related *kyogen farce*, it evolved from various popular, folk and aristocratic art forms, including Dengaku, Shirabyoshi and Gagaku. Although Noh has been slow and stylized for several centuries, its roots can be traced back to Chinese theatre, Sarugaku and folk theatricals.

Numerology is any of many systems, traditions or beliefs in a mystical or esoteric relationship between numbers and physical objects or living things. Numerology and numerological divination were popular among early mathematicians, such as Pythagoras, but are no longer considered part of mathematics and are regarded as pseudomathematics by most modern scientists. Numerology is the study of the occult meanings of numbers and their influence on human life.

Otherness (the other) is the concept in opposition to the same, or other to what is being considered. It is associated with postcolonial discourses and issues of political and cultural identity. The term 'other' usually refers to a person who is signalled out as being different or whose opinion/position is other to the one of the self or own culture. The idea of otherness extends to society (culture), and comes out of the concept where 'other' is defined in regard to the mainstream, or being other to the one dominant cultural or political centre. The term has particular relevance in cultural studies and discussions about individual and group identity within the postcolonial theatre discourse.

Piaget, Jean (1896–1980) was a Swiss philosopher and developmental psychologist. His work on cognitive development and study of children pioneered the constructive theory of knowledge.

Planchon, Roger (1931–) is a French theatre director, actor and playwright. He is one of the main exponents of the idea that the director is a stage writer, referring to *mise-en-scène* as *écriture* *scénique*. After early productions of the plays of Arthur Adamov and Bertolt Brecht, he established a theatre company in Villeurbanne, outside Lyon, France, in 1957. It became the Théâtre National Populaire in 1973. Some of Planchon's major productions include Shakespeare's *Henry V* (1957), Molière's *Tartuffe* (1962 and 1973), Harold Pinter's *No Man's Land* (1979), and Jean-Baptiste Racine's *Athalie* (1980).

Postmodern is a cultural, philosophical and artistic phenomenon that applies to a wide range of disciplines. It is generally defined as emerging in response to modernism, either as a reaction or a next step in the development of modernism. Some of the key characteristics of postmodernism are subjectivity, variety of perceptions of the artwork, absence of a grand narrative, blurring distinction between genres and styles, fragmentation, randomness, collages of different material, rejection of distinction between popular and high culture.

Quebec's nationalist politics is inseparable from the history of Quebec as a French colony that was occupied by the British Empire in 1760, imposing its rule on the majority francophone population. Modern nationalism in Quebec in the post-1960s Quiet Revolution period had a detrimental role in the development of Quebec's national theatre and film. Cultural self-awareness and a cosmopolitan multi-cultural society in the second part of the twentieth century changed the face of Quebec as a nation dominated by white French Catholics to one that has a consciousness of being a modern plural nation, consisting of multiple cultures.

Schechner, Richard (1934–) is one of the founders of the discipline of Performance Studies, extending theatre principles to everyday life and exploring the laws of rituals and ceremonies as performance. In the 1960s he founded The Performance Group, an experimental collective theatre group. Schechner is a Professor of Performance Studies at the Tisch School of the Arts, New York University. He founded and is editor of *TDR: The Drama Review*, and is artistic director of East Coast Artists.

Stein, Peter (1937–) is an internationally critically acclaimed German theatre and opera director who established himself at the Schaubühne am Lehniner Platz, a company he arguably brought to the forefront of German theatre. He combines the actors' collective approach with a strong director's vision. Stein is renowned for his innovative approach to classic plays – his interpretation of Anton Chekov's *The Seagull* is considered to be a landmark staging.

Strindberg, August (1849–1912) was a Swedish playwright, novelist and short-story writer. He is credited as the father of modern drama, working within the styles of Naturalism and later Expressionism. *Miss Julie, The Damascus Trilogy* and *A Dream Play* are generally considered to have been his most influential on contemporary theatre, through mixing personal impression, dream-like events and reality.

Total theatre is a concept put forward at the beginning of the twentieth century by English theatre visionary, director and designer Edward Gordon Craig. The main focus of total theatre is on integration or combination of arts on stage to create one unified aesthetic expression. In total theatre the space and the actors' movements are connected, and stage meaning is created equally through lights, colours, visual images, movement and music as well as through dialogue and spoken text. The main idea behind total theatre that is relevant today is that it liberates performance from servitude to text, and allows all production elements to have equal representational value.

Wagner, Wilhelm Richard (1813–83) was a German composer, music theorist and essayist, known for his operas (or 'music drama' as he called them). Wagner wrote his own scenarios and librettos. He transformed opera and theatre through his idea of *gesamtkunstwerk* (total artwork) – the synthesis of all the poetic, visual, musical and dramatic arts, epitomized by his monumental four-opera cycle *Der Ring des Nibelungen* (1876). Wagner even went so far as to build his own opera-house to try to stage these works as he had imagined them.

Wilson, Robert (1941–) is a theatre author, director and designer. He is a pioneer of the theatre of images, emphasizing spatial composition, music and performers' movement. He has collaborated with a range of important artists including Philip Glass, William S. Burroughs, Allen Ginsberg, Tom Waits and David Byrne. In 1968 Wilson founded an experimental performance company, the Byrd Hoffman School of Byrds. With this company he created his first major works, beginning with 1969's *The*

King of Spain and *The Life and Times of Sigmund Freud*. He began to work in opera in the early 1970s, creating *Einstein on the Beach* with Philip Glass, which brought the two artists worldwide fame.

Yin and yang are ancient Chinese philosophy symbols for antithesis, for two opposing principles. Under yang we find the principles of masculinity (sun, light, dominance), while yin represents female aspects (moon, darkness, submission).

BIBLIOGRAPHY

Appia, Adolphe (1962). *Music and the Art of Theatre.* Translated by Robert W. Corrigan and Mary Douglas Dirks. Coral Gables, Fla.: University of Miami Press.

Augé, Marc (1995). *Non-Places: Introduction to an Anthropology of Supermodernity* London: Verso.

Auslander, Philip (1999). *Liveness.* London: Routledge.

Barker, Clive (1989). *Theatre Games: A New Approach to Drama Training.* London: Methuen.

Barthes, Roland (1993). *Mythologies.* Translated by Annette Laverse. London: Vintage Classics.

Beauchamp, Hélène (1990). 'Appartenance et territoires: Repères chronologiques.' *L'Annuaire théâtral* 8: 41–72.

Bennett, Susan (1994). *Theatre Audience: A Theory of Production and Reception.* London: Routledge.

Bharucha, Rustom (1993). *Theatre and the World.* London: Routledge.

Bial, Henry, ed. (2004). *The Performance Studies Reader.* London: Routledge.

Blankenship, Rebecca (1996). Interview by author. Tape recording. October. London.

Bradby, David (1991). *Modern French Drama*. Cambridge: Cambridge University Press.

Bradby, David and David Williams (1988). *Directors' Theatre*. London: Macmillan Press.

Bradby, David and Annie Sparks (1997). *Mise-en-scène: French Theatre Now.* London: Methuen.

Brassard, Marie (1996). Interview by author. Tape recording. October. London.

Brook, Peter (1968). *The Empty Space*. Harmondsworth: Penguin.

———(1987). *The Shifting Point*. London: Methuen.

Bunzli, James (1999). 'The Geography of Creation.' *The Drama Review* 43 (Spring): 79–103.

Burian, Jarka (1971). *The Scenography of Josef Svoboda*. Middletown, Conn.: Wesleyan University Press.

Carson, Christie (1993). 'Collaboration, Translation, Interpretation.' *New Theatre Quarterly* 33 (February): 31–36.

Chamberlain, Franc and Yarrow, Ralph, eds. (2002). *Jacques Lecoq and the British Theatre*. London: Routledge.

Charest, Rémy (1997). *Robert Lepage: Connecting Flights*. Translated by Wanda Romer Taylor. London: Methuen.

———(2006). '*Connecting Flights* ten years after.' Edited by Aleksandar Dundjerović. Paper presented at the International Conference on Robert Lepage, London, 1–3 June.

Cocteau, Jean (1994). *The Art of Cinema*. Edited by André Bernard and Claude Gauteur. London: Marion Boyars.

Delgado, Maria M. and Paul Heritage, eds. (1996). *In Contact with the Gods? Directors Talk Theatre*. Manchester: Manchester University Press.

Dixon, Steve (2007). *Digital Performance: A History of New Media in Theatre, Dance, Performance Art and Installation*. Cambridge, Mass.: MIT Press.

Donohoe, Joseph, Jr. and Jane Koustas, eds. (2000). *Theater sans frontières: Essays on the Dramatic Universe of Robert Lepage*. East Lansing: Michigan State University Press.

Donohoe, Joseph, Jr. and Jonathan Weiss, eds. (1997). *Essays on Modern Quebec Theatre*. East Lansing: Michigan State University Press.

Dundjerović, Aleksandar (2003). *The Cinema of Robert Lepage: The Poetics of Memory*. London: Wallflower Press.

——(2003a). 'The Multiple Crossings to *The Far Side of the Moon*: Transformative Mise-en-scène.' *Contemporary Theatre Review* 13, no. 2: 67–82.

——(2007). *The Theatricality of Robert Lepage*. Montreal: McGill-Queen's University Press.

Etchells, Tim (1999). *Certain Fragments: Texts and Writings on Performance*. London: Routledge.

Fouquet, Ludovic (2005). *Robert Lepage: L'Horizon en images*. Quebec City: L'Instant Même.

Fricker, Karen (2003). 'Tourism, the Festival Marketplace and Robert Lepage's *The Seven Streams of the River Ota*.' *Contemporary Theatre Review* 13, no. 4 (Fall): 79–93.

Gignac, Marie (1987). 'Points de repère.' *Jeu* 45: 177–82.

Goffman, Erving (1959). *The Presentation of the Self in Everyday Life*. Harmondsworth: Penguin.

Goldberg, RoseLee (1999). *Performance Art*. London: Thames & Hudson.

Guilfoyle, Tony (2006). Interview by author. Tape recording. October. London.

Halprin, Anna (2000). *Dance as a Healing Art: Returning to Health through Movement and Imagery*. Mendocino CA: Life Rhythm.

Halprin, Lawrence (1969). *The RSVP Cycles: Creative Processes in the Human Environment*. New York: George Braziller.

Heddon, Deirdre and Jane Milling (2006). *Devising Performance: A Critical History*. New York: Palgrave Macmillan.

Hemming, Sarah (1991). 'Conjuring Act.' *Independent* (London), 30 October.

Hodge, Alison, ed. (2000). *Twentieth Century Actor Training*. London: Routledge.

Hunt, Nigel (1989). 'The Global Voyage of Robert Lepage.' *The Drama Review* 33 (Summer): 104–18.

Hutcheon, Linda (1989). *The Politics of Post-modernism*. London: Routledge.

Huxley, Michael and Noel Witts, eds. (1996). *The Twentieth-Century Performance Reader*. London: Routledge.

Jacobson, Lynn (1991). 'Tectonic States.' *American Theatre Journal*. November: 16–22.

Jencks, Charles (1989). *What is Post-modernism?* 3rd ed. London: St Martin's Press.

Jeu (1987) 'Reconstruction de la *Trilogie*.' 45, no. 4: the whole issue.

Johnstone, Keith (1987). *Impro: Improvisation and the Theatre*. New York: Theatre Art Books.

——(1999). *Impro for Storytellers*. New York: Routledge/Theatre Art Books.

Jung, Carl Gustav (1966). *The Spirit in Man, Art, and Literature*. Translated by R.F.C. Hull. vol. 15, *The Collected Works of C.G. Jung* London: Routledge & Kegan Paul.

——ed. (1978). *Man and His Symbols*. London: Aldus.

——(1979). Foreword to *I Ching: The Book of Change*. Edited by Dan Baruth. Translated by John Blofield. Visited on www.iging.com/intro/foreword.htm

Kaye, Nick (1994). *Postmodernism and Performance*. London: Macmillan.

Knapp, Alain (1992). 'Pour une autre pédagogie du théâtre: Entretien avec Alain Knapp.' Interview by Josette Féral. In *Jeu* 63: 55–64.

Lavender, Andy (2001). *Hamlet in Pieces: Shakespeare Reworked by Peter Brook, Robert Lepage, Robert Wilson*. London: Nick Hern.

Lecoque, Jacques (2001). *The Moving Body: Teaching Creative Theatre*. Translated by David Bradby. London: Routledge.

Lefebvre, Paul (1987). 'Robert Lepage: New Filters for Creation.' *Canadian Theatre Review* 52 (Fall): 30–35.

Lepage, Robert (1991). Interview by Christi Carson. Tape recording. National Arts Centre, Ottawa.

——(1992). 'Robert Lepage in Discussion.' Interview by Richard Eyre. In Huxley and Witts, *The Twentieth-Century Performance Reader*, 237–47.

——(1999). Interview by author. Tape recording. December. Quebec City.

——(2002). Interview by author. Tape recording. January. Quebec City.

——(2005). Interview by author. Notes. July. Quebec City.

——(2005). *La Trilogie des Dragons* (The Dragons' Trilogy) Montréal: L'instant sine.

Lepage, Robert and Ex Machina (1997). *The Seven Streams of the River Ota*. London: Methuen.

Lepage, Robert and Marie Brassard (2003). *Polygraph*. London: A&C Black.

Lyotard, Jean-François (1992). 'What is Post-modernism.' In *The Post-modern Reader*, edited by Charles Jencks, 138–50. London: Academy.

McAlpine, Allison (1996). 'Robert Lepage.' in *In Contact with the Gods? Directors Talk Theatre*, edited by Maria M. Delgado and Paul Heritage, 130–57. Manchester: Manchester University Press.

McAuley, Gay (2000). *Space in Performance: Making Meaning in the Theatre*. Ann Arbor: University of Michigan Press.

Machor, James and Philip Goldstein, eds. (2000). *Reception Study: From Literary Theory to Cultural Studies*. London: Routledge.

Melzner, Annabelle (1994). *Dada and Surrealist Performance*. Baltimore: Johns Hopkins University Press.

Mirzoeff, Nicholas (1999). *An Introduction to Visual Culture*. London: Routledge.

Mitter, Shomit (1992). *Systems of Rehearsal*. London: Routledge.

Oddey, Alison (1994). *Devising Theatre: A Practical and Theoretical Handbook*. London: Routledge.

Pavis, Patrice (1992). *Theatre at the Crossroads of Culture*. London: Routledge.

——ed. (1996). *The Intercultural Performance Reader*. London: Routledge.

Piaget, Jean (1951). *Play, Dreams and Imitation in Childhood*. Translated by C. Gattegno and F.M. Hodgson. Melbourne: Heinemann, in association with the New Education Fellowship.

———(1955). *The Child's Construction of Reality.* London: Routledge & Kegan Paul.

Piaget, Jean and Barbel Inherdel (2000). *The Psychology of the Child.* New York: Basic Books.

Postlewait, Thomas and Davis C. Tracy (2003). *Theatricality.* Cambridge: Cambridge University Press.

Quick, Andrew (2007). *The Wooster Group Work Book.* London: Routledge.

Radz, Matt (2002). 'Strobe-lit Spectacle,' *Gazette* (Montreal), 28 June. www.canada.com/montrealgazette/index.html

Rewa, Natalie (1990). 'Cliches of Ethnicity Subverted: Robert Lepage's "La Trilogie des Dragons".' *Theatre History in Canada* 11, no. 2 (Fall): 148–61.

Roy, Irène (1990). 'Robert Lepage et L'esthétique en contrepoint.' *L'Annuaire théâtral.* 8: 73–80.

———(1993). *Le Théâtre Repère: Du ludique au poétique dans le théâtre de recherche.* Quebec City: Nuit Blanche.

Said, Edward (1991). *Orientalism.* Harmondsworth: Penguin.

Schechner, Richard (2002). *Performance Studies.* London: Routledge.

Schechner, Richard and Willa Appel, eds. (1991). *By Means of Performance: Intercultural Studies of Theatre and Ritual.* Cambridge: Cambridge University Press.

Steegmuller, Francis (1970). *Cocteau: A Biography.* London: Macmillan.

Svich, Caridad, ed. (2003). *Trans-Global Readings: Crossing Theatrical Boundaries.* Manchester: Manchester University Press.

Wallace, Robert (1990). *Producing Marginality-Theatre and Criticism in Canada.* Saskatoon: Fifth House.

Whitley, John (1999). 'A Passion for Unpolished Gems.' *Daily Telegraph* (London), 6 March: 23.

Worth, Libby (2005). 'Anna Halprin in Paris.' *Contemporary Theatre Review* 15, no. 4: 440–48.

VIDEO/FILM LIST

Brook, Peter (1992). *De l'espace vide au théâtre sacré.* video by J.-G. Carasso and Mohamed Charbagi. CICT/Anrat video cassette.

Gabriel, Peter (1994). *Secret World Live*, DVD. Los Angeles: Universal Music & Video Distribution.

Lepage, Robert (2003). *The Far Side of the Moon.* Film on DVD.

——(1998). *No.* Film on DVD.

——(1995). *Confessional.* Film on DVD.

Les plaques tectoniques/Tectonic Plates (1993). Dir. Peter Mettler. Videocassette. Toronto: Hauer Rawlence Productions.

Who Is This Nobody from Quebec? (1992). Dir. Debra Hauer. BFI Video.

USEFUL WEBSITES

http://lacaserne.net/index2.php/lacaserne/intro/

www.bbc.co.uk/radio3/johntusainterview/lepage_transcript.shtml

http://www.youtube.com/watch?v=sqhUSm451gI
Robert Lepage: 'Performing Past and Present' (14 Nov 2007). Online video.

INDEX

Note: Page numbers in **bold** refer to figures.

Augusto Boal

Routledge Performance Practitioners series

Frances Babbage

The work of Augusto Boal has had a tremendous impact on contemporary theatre. This volume looks at the scope of Boal's career –
from his early work as a playwright and director in Sao Paulo in the
1950s, to the development of his groundbreaking manifesto in the
1970s for a 'Theatre of the Oppressed'.

Augusto Boal will be fascinating reading for anyone interested in the
role that theatre can play in stimulating social and personal change.
This useful study combines:

- a biographical and historical overview of Boal's career as theatre
  practitioner and director
- in-depth analysis of Boal's classic text on radical theatre, *The
  Theatre of the Oppressed*
- exploration of training and production techniques
- practical guidance to Boal's workshop methods.

As a first step towards critical understanding, and as an initial
exploration before going on to further, primary research, *Routledge
Performance Practitioners* are unbeatable value for today's student.

ISBN13: 978-0-415-27325-1 (hbk)
ISBN13: 978-0-415-27326-8 (pbk)
ISBN13: 978-0-203-30900-1 (ebk)

Anna Halprin

Routledge Performance Practitioners series

Libby Worth and Helen Poynor

This guidebook traces the life's work of radical dance-maker Anna Halprin, documenting her early career as a modern dancer in the 1940s through to the development of her groundbreaking approach to dance as an accessible and life-enhancing art form. Tracing the evolution of the San Francisco Dancers' Workshop, it explores Halprin's connections with the avant-garde theatre, music, visual art and architecture of the 1950s and 60s, and analyses her work from this period.

Anna Halprin not only offers a useful introduction to the life and work of this major figure, but also provides an important historical guide to a time when dance was first explored beyond the confines of the theatre and considered as a healing art for individuals and communities.

As a first step towards critical understanding, and as an initial exploration before going on to further, primary research, *Routledge Performance Practitioners* are unbeatable value for today's student.

ISBN13: 978-0-415-27329-9 (hbk)
ISBN13: 978-0-415-27330-5 (pbk)
ISBN13: 978-0-203-30792-2 (ebk)

Related titles from Routledge

Mary Wigman

Routledge Performance Practitioners series

Mary Anne Santos Newhall

All books in the *Routledge Performance Practitioners* series are carefully designed to enable the reader to understand the work of a key practitioner. They provide the first step towards critical understanding and a springboard for further study for students on twentieth century, contemporary theatre and theatre history courses.

A dancer, teacher and choreographer, Mary Wigman was a leading innovator in expressionist dance. Her radical explorations of movement and dance theory are credited with expanding the scope of dance as a theatrical art in her native Germany and beyond. This book combines for the first time:

- a full account of Wigman's life and work;
- detailed discussion of her aesthetic theories, including the use of space as an 'invisible partner' and the transcendent nature of performance;
- a commentary on her key works, including *Hexentantz* and *The Seven Dances of Life*; and
- an extensive collection of practical exercises designed to provide an understanding of Wigman's choreographic principles and her uniquely immersive approach to dance.

ISBN13: 978-0-415-37526-9 (hbk)
ISBN13: 978-0-415-37527-6 (pbk)

Available at all good bookshops
For ordering and further information please visit:
www.routledge.com